Teaching Under Pressure:
Looking at primary teachers' stress

Anne D. Cockburn

> *Teaching makes many immense demands on the mind and feelings of the teacher. There is constant danger of overload, and the teacher must be aware of the hazards of personal stress.*
> *(Laar, 1989, p.42)*

With illustrations by Peter Kent

Falmer Press

(A member of the Taylor & Francis Group)
London • Washington, D.C.

USA   The Falmer Press, 4 John St, London WC1N 2ET
UK   The Falmer Press, Taylor & Francis Inc., 1900 Frost Road, Suite 101, Bristol, PA 19007

First published 1996

A catalogue record of this publication is available from the British Library

ISBN 0 7507 0503 5 cased
ISBN 0 7507 0504 3 paper

Library of Congress Cataloging-in-Publication Data are available on request

Jacket design by Caroline Archer

Typeset in 11/13 pt Garamond by
Graphicraft Typesetters Ltd., Hong Kong

Printed in Great Britain by Biddles Ltd, Guildford and King's Lynn on paper which has a specified pH value on final paper manufacture of not less than 7.5 and is therefore 'acid-free'.

Teaching Under Pressure

13.95

To D.B.C. with love, affection and gratitude

Contents

Contents

Contents

Introduction and Acknowledgments

It is to teachers that we entrust our children and thus our future. (Farber, 1991, p.44)

I would assume that it was more stressful than any other job if we're talking about stress being the non-stop demands on you all day long. (Joan, a reception teacher)

This is a book about teachers and the trials and tribulations they face in daily life. It is not full of tales of woe nor, I am afraid, is it the definitive answer to all your problems. Much of it, however, is derived from practising teachers' actions, feelings and thoughts. Some of it you may have heard before, some of it will be entirely new and some of it you may dismiss out of hand. Nevertheless I hope that there is a strong possibility that — for you — it will have succeeded in at least one, if not all, of its three aims:

1 It provides snippets of conversations and text with which you can identify.
2 It introduces possibilities to you, which you may later reject, but which stimulate your thinking towards finding a solution to some of the stresses and strains in your life.
3 It encourages you to explore, and gain greater insight into, what it means to you to be a human being and a teacher.

The book is primarily intended for student teachers, beginning teachers, more experienced teachers and their senior colleagues. It may be seen as a quick skim read. It is also intended to be a more demanding book which invites you to explore yourself, your life and your situation.

Although my name appears on the front cover of *Teaching Under Pressure* the voices of many of your colleagues are found throughout. Some arose as a result of in-depth discussions about teacher stress while others stem from casual remarks made in staffrooms, corridors or yet another professional meeting! All the comments are confidential and therefore, not surprisingly, teachers' names — and sometimes their situations — have been changed. In my view, there is no such person as a 'typical' teacher but, rest assured, the teachers represented here — although unique and talented individuals — are not unusual. Some are young: some are old. Some are highly experienced: others are less so. Some are female but, perhaps a surprising number, are male. Some are noisy, confident extroverts while others are calmer, more placid introverts. Some are headteachers: some are deputies or standard scale teachers. All work extremely hard and — although none appear to be experiencing severe stress — all consider teaching to be a highly demanding and stressful profession. In brief the teachers are like thousands of others throughout the country.

The book is divided into three main sections. The first, 'Understanding and Tackling Stress', is a general introduction to the notion of stress which may provide a useful framework for you when reading later chapters. It is not, however, necessary for you to begin with it as all the chapters are, in essence, free standing. The second and largest section, 'Challenges in Teaching', considers aspects of teachers' professional lives which are often particularly demanding and which frequently induce feelings of stress. The third section, 'Life Beyond Teaching', focuses on the broader issues of life and realizing your potential as we head towards the twenty-first century.

It is never easy writing such a book because it is difficult to get the tone right and pitch it at an appropriate level for everyone. The truth be known it is impossible but, nevertheless, I hope that to some extent I have succeeded in making the book accessible, but not patronizing; valid, but not tediously familiar; and relevant, but not impractical.

To achieve these ends I have many people to thank:

- First and foremost, the many teachers and students who gave of their valuable time to tell me about the stresses and strains in their lives and ways they have tried to alleviate the effects of negative stress. It was a privilege to hear of your personal and professional lives in such detail.
- I would also like to acknowledge the support of the Nuffield Foundation who gave me a grant to undertake this research.
- Grateful thanks are also due to my parents, Richard, Daphne, Anna and Simone for providing useful material and advice.
- And, finally, I would like to thank Liz White and Peter Kent for

converting an illegible scrawl with some vague ideas into a highly professional text with most apposite illustrations.

Anne D. Cockburn
July 1995

Reference

FARBER, B.A. (1991) *Crisis in Education*, San Francisco, Jossey-Bass.

SECTION I
Understanding and Tackling Stress

This section focuses on stress in general terms. It considers the types of negative stress we most commonly experience and explores a variety of strategies for coping with the stresses and strains in our everyday lives.

1   Sussing Out Stress

Children and teachers are not plastic and cannot be moulded . . .
They mould themselves from what they are and from what they
wish to become in the context of the opportunities and constraints they experience. (Hutchinson, 1989, p.160)

Introduction

Stress can be positively good for you. Indeed, without a certain amount
of stress in our lives, most of us would die of boredom. Imagine a
world without the excitement of falling in love, the pleasures of the first
spring day, the laughter of a joyous moment, or the thrill of . . . (flying/
sailing/driving at high speeds or whatever else turns you on). What a
tedious place it would be! Stress — or 'distress' as it is often perceived
— can, however, present real problems for many people. In this chapter we will explore the nature of negative stress and begin to examine
some of the ways in which it can be alleviated.

Types of Stress

It seems to me that there are five main categories of stress. Differenti-
ating between them can provide a useful starting point for analysing
the negative aspects of stress in our lives. The first, and most obvious,
is that you find yourself in a situation — an examination, a heated
argument or dangling over the side of a cliff, for example — which
proves stressful for you. In shorthand this could be considered 'here
and now stress'.

A second type of stress is a reaction to an anticipated event. The
thought of a parents' evening, a driving test or a parachute jump, for
example, might send you into a panic. In other words it is the 'stress
of anticipation'.

The third category of stress is down to your imagination but none
the less nerve-racking because of it. Your imagination might transport
you to a terrifying situation shown on the television. You might be

alone at night, hear a noise and conjure up all sorts of frightening possibilities. Or you might simply be sitting in an armchair picturing what the world might be like if everyone became violently aggressive and egocentric. We could call this 'imaginative stress'.

Negative stress can also arise from events in the past. It can take a variety of forms and, at its most extreme, might manifest itself in post-traumatic stress syndrome. Grief is often associated with this type of stress, be it as the result of a bereavement or your imagining what might have been 'if only . . .'. 'Reactive stress' can be a very natural and necessary part of the healing process. If, however, it becomes a frequent attempt to 'rearrange the past' whenever anything goes even slightly wrong, it can be very wearing and even destructive.

The final category of stress is rather different in type. This is the negative stress which generally builds up over a period of days, weeks or even years. It may be attributable to a single, fairly easily defined source (e.g., never having enough money) or it may originate from a web of more diverse and opaque origins. Much of what follows may be applied directly to, or slightly adapted for, cases of chronic stress. Most of the examples, however, will illustrate more immediate, short-term situations — in part because they are more commonly experienced by the majority of teachers and partly because they are often the introductory components of chronic stress.

I suspect we all suffer from all five types of stress at various times in our lives but the frequency and severity of each will be unique to us as individuals. Knowing the type of stress you are experiencing can be an important first step to tackling it. This often, however, appears to be deceptively simple.

Unravelling Our Stress

It may be relatively easy to list a whole host of thoughts and incidents which have created anxiety during the course of a day: the children acted up, there simply was not enough time to do everything, the thought of your next appraisal kept looming up, and so on and so forth. These may all have been real problems but the bottom line might be that the underlying cause of your stress is something else again. It could be that you were exhausted: being tired makes you more prone to feelings of stress, you are less alert and more disorganized, creating a less efficient — and hence probably more boring — learning environment in which neither you nor your pupils display your true potential. And this in turn creates more stress. . .

Or how often have you found people really irritating and wanted to snap their heads off? It may be that they are incredibly tiresome or it may be that you are quite simply hungry. This might sound ridiculous to many but next time you find yourself getting very steamed up over a respected colleague's behaviour note the time of day and the state of your stomach!

A third, and final, illustration of how your lifestyle can induce seemingly unwarranted or unexpected stress reactions to situations is to consider your consumption of coffee, sugar and even salt. Too much of these can alter the physiological balances within your body (e.g., by increasing your heart rate or blood pressure) and thus make you more susceptible to stress.

It may be, however, that some of you are more prone to stress than others for more fundamental reasons. Two of these are relatively well documented — personality types and, for want of a better term, naturally induced phenomena. Research of the first — personality type — suggests that individuals may very broadly be defined as Type A personalities or Type B personalities, the former being more susceptible to stress than the latter. More specifically Type A personalities tend to be very hard-working, competitive people who find it hard to relax and are prone to heart disease and strokes. They invariably find that there is never enough time to get everything done and tasks are often left to the last minute and completed (when things are going well!) at the eleventh hour. They frequently enjoy the positive stresses of life but they also suffer from the more negative aspects induced by overwork and panic. In contrast Type B personalities tend to be far more equable, calm and easy-going. They are not highly ambitious, do not live for their work and are less at risk from stress and heart disease. Few people fall neatly into one personality category or the other; occasionally you will find someone who is a perfect balance of the two but, although a blend, the majority of us exhibit personality traits which predominatly describe one type or the other. Acknowledging and gaining greater understanding of your unique personality type can be an important step in recognizing the — dare I say — raw material with which you are working.

Unlike personality types (unless you have been affected by illness or drugs) naturally induced phenomena may make you more prone to stress at certain times of your life, the menopause being a well documented case in point. Other examples include cyclical susceptibility brought about when suffering from seasonal affective disorder (SAD). In such cases individuals become more and more depressed as the days become shorter and the winter nights draw in. As this condition is becoming more understood it is increasingly recognized that special lighting can significantly alleviate the symptoms. Should you be, or discover, therefore, that you are more susceptible to stress at certain times of the day, week, month or year than others it may well be worth your following the matter up with your doctor. It may be SAD you are experiencing but there may well be another physiological explanation which could prove amenable to simple intervention.

By now you may be feeling totally frustrated and wondering why on earth you are spending your time on this book. Of course people suffer from stress for all the above reasons but you already know perfectly well what is stressing you and you want to know what to do about it! So what are the possibilities?

Stress Strategies

It seems to me that there are ten general ways in which to approach stress. They are not mutually exclusive and, indeed, it may often be appropriate to start with one and then move on to another. The initial strategy will depend on a number of factors, such as whether you have time to reflect — and so choose — your response; what sort of person you are; possible implications for you and other involved parties; and, of course, the situation itself. If possible, a wise precaution is to pay heed to your susceptibilities before adopting a suggestion wholesale. For example, a classic technique when dealing with stress is to consider what is the worst thing that could happen in a specific situation — a school assembly perhaps. Should you be particularly prone to imaginative stress, however, this is probably not a good idea! Returning to stress strategies. . .

Reduce the Odds

The aim and, in later chapters, the focus of this book is to reduce the odds of your becoming negatively stressed in the first place. Unfortunately there are no fool-proof, one-off answers though there are insurance policies you can adopt in your daily life. Some of the most successful of these are outlined in Figure 1.1 and will be referred to again later in the book. By way of explanation, however, I will briefly outline what I mean by some of my shorthand. As I do so it will become clear that the strategies are not necessarily mutually exclusive.

Apart from the sheer pleasure of having friends and colleagues whom you like to be with it is important to remember that situations

Figure 1.1: Some insurance policies for reducing the stress in your life

change and that, now and again, relationships require systems maintenance. For example, supposing someone you can really talk to emigrates, is there anyone else with whom you can discuss this and that? Or, over the years, have friends fallen by the wayside because you have not seen or written to them in ages? Having good close relationships often enables you to explore the day's events and all manner of other issues in a way that can clarify situations without them ever becoming noticeable sources of stress. For example, you might describe and laugh about a staffroom incident rather than allow it to fester away in the confines of your mind. Such friends can also be an important source of support in more trying times.

Having regular exercise can indeed make your body work more efficiently and reduce the likelihood of stress. On the other hand, it might induce stress and prove totally counter-productive. It may take time and effort (see Chapter 8) but it is worth finding some form of realistic exercise which will help keep your body and mind in good health.

It is important that every day you take some time — it need not be very long — to yourself. Go for a five minute walk in a local park at lunchtime or bury yourself in a book for a few minutes perhaps. Such times can be extremely restorative and enable you to switch off and be yourself — rather than a teacher, cook, partner, etc. — for a short time. Often overlapping with this suggestion is escaping: take time out from 'the real world' now and again and you will almost certainly feel the better for it (unless of course you make an unfortunate choice of book . . .)

Recognizing your priorities can sometimes take tremendous pressure off your life. If, for example, you decide that the family comes first and one day your child falls ill there will be no need for agonizing — quite simply you take the day off school.

And, finally, enjoying life seems to be remarkably straightforward for some but distinctly less so for others. In Chapter 8 we will return to the issue.

Ignore It

Simply ignoring the cause(s) of your stress may sometimes be your best policy. For example, if Johnnie and Mary are being particularly tiresome during story time, try ignoring them (unless they are causing injury to another child) and you may find that they become bored and settle down to listen to the story.

Such tactical ignoring can be a useful ploy for some but, for others, ignoring their stress may well be denying its very existence. Popular books and magazines often pose key questions designed to identify those under stress and winkle out those who may be ignoring it. What, for example, are your immediate responses to the following:

- Do you sometimes find it difficult to 'switch off' from work?
- Do you suffer from insomnia or do you often wake up in the early hours of the morning worrying?
- Do you burst into tears at the slightest provocation?
- Do you frequently feel irritable?
- Do you often suffer from indigestion or poor appetite?
- Do you panic when in crowds or confined spaces?
- Do you find it more difficult to make decisions than you used to?
- Do you experience feelings of hopelessness?

Answering 'yes' to one or more of these questions may mean you are experiencing chronic stress. In the short term this may be relatively harmless but in the longer term it will undoubtedly begin to affect your health, not to mention the quality of your life. A constructive solution is not to panic but calmly to assess which of the following options may be realistic for you and your situation. Alternatively a sympathetic doctor may be your first port of call.

Avoid It

Another way to tackle stress is simply to avoid it whenever possible. This can sometimes be relatively straightforward. For example, why go to a party if you know your ex-partner will be there? Why volunteer to take on yet another chore when you have plenty to keep you going? I strongly suspect that this is a strategy too frequently adopted by some people and not adopted often enough by others. The latter group tend to be highly conscientious individuals who are apt to feel guilty if they do not take on every available task and weak when they do not con-front every difficult situation. I'll warrant that at least nine out of ten people reading this book fall into this category!

In contrast, some people spend their lives avoiding demands and taxing situations. By doing so they deny themselves the opportunity to mature and develop, added to which they may be missing out on much of what life has to offer.

Remove Yourself from It

Whatever type of stress you are suffering from it will almost invariably be possible to remove yourself from it figuratively, temporarily or permanently. One of the few situations where this might not be possible is if you find yourself fully aware, but unable to move a muscle, on the operating table. Fortunately, a recent article in the paper suggests that this horrendous possibility may soon be a thing of the past.

So how do you 'figuratively' remove yourself from a roomful of noisy belligerent 10 year olds? Quite simply — and, unfortunately, of necessity extremely briefly — switch off and let your mind transport you to a more conducive environment. A sun-drenched beach by the Pacific perhaps? Or maybe that cosy little bistro down the road where you enjoyed a meal the other night? Such fleeting flights of fantasy can prove remarkably restorative, but try to ensure that a major fight does not start up while you are blissfully enjoying your trip.

A more major step is temporarily to physically remove yourself from the stressful situation in which you find yourself. In the stress-inducing classroom you could leave the room for a short time. This is obviously not a strategy to be taken lightly and ideally you would send a responsible pupil to fetch another teacher to cover for you before you make your departure. At the very least, you should fetch someone yourself as you are leaving, otherwise your actions may result in chaos not to say the possibility of losing your job! Many of you are unlikely to adopt this option but you may find it comforting to know that you have a choice when next confronted with a diabolical situation.

Should you decide to leave the classroom — particularly if you are a student, new to teaching or particularly distressed — it would almost certainly be a good idea to talk your actions over with a sympathetic confidante shortly afterwards. Such a strategy also applies to other situations where your actions may result in feelings of guilt or loss of confidence.

A variation on removing yourself from a source of stress is to remove the source of stress from you. A common practice in many schools is to swap 'difficult' pupils with a colleague from time to time. That way you can have some necessary relief and you can return the favour when you are feeling more cheerful and positive.

On the domestic front, a way to obtain temporary relief from an ailing partnership or grouchy children might be to set a couple of hours aside for yourself every now and again — a night out with friends, an evening class or even a holiday.

More radically you can permanently remove yourself from the

source of stress. Ideally this decision should never be taken lightly nor without consulting people who might be affected or individuals who might be able to help you reach an appropriate decision. Just knowing that you *can* leave your job, your partner or the dentist's chair can prove enormously liberating. You may never take such actions but you have the freedom, and the right, to do so if you so choose. Initially thoughts of money, security, respectability and so on may enter your head but, at the end of the day, life is short. Obviously if you can avoid hurting anyone in the process — or at least minimize their hurt — so much the better.

Acknowledge Your Needs and Anticipate

People can often be accused of being selfish if they take time to consider themselves and their needs. It may well be that they are being egocentric and spoilt or it may be that they are acknowledging their needs as they take into consideration the needs of others. For example, you may find that you feel drained when you come home from work. By taking twenty minutes on your own with the latest potboiler, however, you may find yourself restored and ready to listen to the trials and tribulations of someone else's day. Acknowledging your needs in this way can often be a way of dissipating the stresses of the day and reducing the likelihood of further stressful situations arising. Another well recognized way to do this is to take physical exercise but, as discussed, this may not be to your taste (see Chapter 8).

Acknowledging your needs, in some situations, need have no direct impact on others. For example, if you know that you have a tendency to become hot and bothered in stressful situations, wear layers in the best hiker's tradition. Next time you have someone watching you teach, therefore, you can remove your top layer rather than quietly boiling away in your woolly jumper. If you know you have a hopeless memory, write things down rather than struggling to cram your head full of important things to remember.

Such strategies involve having an awareness of you and the situation you are about to face. This knowledge can prove tremendously helpful when dealing with a wide variety of situations. It usually comes through insight and experience and the subject will be taken up again in Chapter 8. It is important to recognize, however, that sometimes this solution may be quickly and easily put into operation and other times it might take far longer. For example, if you are a relatively meek and mild person you may find it extremely stressful having to state your point of view and, if necessary, stand your ground at staff meetings. It is unlikely the circumstances will change overnight but, by enrolling in an assertiveness class, you may well find that in due course you are generally more confident and better able to respond in all manner of situations.

Compartmentalize

Compartmentalizing is, I suspect, something that most busy people become, of necessity, very good at: you simply can't worry about the curious noise the car was making when you have thirty 5 year olds clamouring for your attention.

Other people compartmentalize their lives without really thinking about it but, sometimes, a concerted effort may be called for. A student of mine is in the midst of preparing for her wedding at the same time as battling her way through our highly demanding teacher training course. She is quite clear, however:

> When I came to the university I put my wedding plans to one side. It's quite hard but I have to do it otherwise I'd never get any work done!

Should you find it impossible to compartmentalize it may well be that the problem you are trying to put to one side for the time being is more serious than you thought and, in fact, merits your immediate attention. Susan found this when her 16-year-old daughter was ill:

> Normally if she has a mild dose of flu I am quite happy to leave her at home on her own but recently she seemed exceptionally poorly and I knew that my time would be better spent with her than being a wet blanket at school.

Some might be shocked at the idea of taking such a day off school but I would argue that it is important to get your priorities right otherwise you may simply be creating considerable reactive stress for the future.

Acknowledge and Live with the Situation

At one time or another we all have to face stressful situations whether we like it or not: a classic example being a visit to the dentist. There may be very little we can do to lessen our stress (although, in reality, this is rarely the case) and the best policy may well be simply to grit your teeth and get on with it — sooner rather than later if possible — the exception being, of course, when you are at the dentist's in which case your actions have to be mental rather than physical.

Gritting your teeth can, to some extent, lessen feelings of stress, as can thoughts that the situation is finite and, as discussed, the knowledge that in 99 per cent of cases you have the freedom actually to remove yourself from it. In my view, sometimes you should just forget 'putting a brave face on it'. As it happens, if you feel nervous in an interview you would almost invariably create a better impression if you actually said, 'I am afraid I am rather nervous', rather than stuttering and spluttering away. If things are too much perhaps a good cry really is the answer, although it may not be the most effective strategy in the example just described!

Tackling stress by living with it, however, is only really recommended for short-term, one-off stressful situations. Adopting such a policy for any longer may well prove injurious to your health and prevent you exploring other possible options.

Reduce the Physical Sensations

On finding themselves in acutely stressful situations people generally adopt the 'fight or flight response': their heart rate speeds up, they start to sweat, their stomach churns, their muscles tense, their breathing becomes faster and shallower, and they get themselves ready for action just as their ancestors did thousands of years ago (see Figure 1.2). In brief, within seconds, you can find yourself remarkably uncomfortable. There are a number of simple strategies to relieve the situation.

Wherever you are — unless it is underwater — you can usually make a conscious effort to breathe more slowly. This helps correct the balance of carbon dioxide in your body and reduces the possibility of dizziness, palpitations and sweating. It also makes you feel calmer! Another generally helpful ploy is to make your body more relaxed by, for example, unclenching your fingers and dropping your jaw slightly (to stop yourself from grinding your teeth). If you are sitting down sit back in the chair rather than remain perching on the edge of it. If you are standing up — and circumstances permit — walk about a bit. This will help relax your muscles. If you are talking, slow the pace. It is almost as if you are turning off your body's response to stress, allowing the organs to regenerate and function normally once more. Indeed, this strategy can sometimes prove so effective that, to my surprise, I have sometimes found myself quite enjoying job interviews!

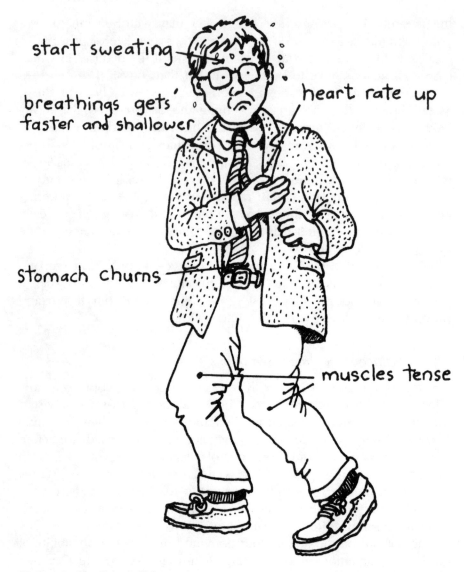

start sweating

breathings gets faster and shallower

heart rate up

Stomach churns

muscles tense

Figure 1.2: The fight or flight response to stress

Taking this strategy a step further — which is really beyond the scope of this book — it is possible to use biofeedback techniques to minimize the body's 'fight or flight' response in stressful situations. On a less sophisticated level, apparently — but I have never tested this — if you think you are about to cry and you really screw your face up, your tears can be put on hold until a more appropriate time. Having said that, any spectators may fall about laughing at your weird and wonderful facial expressions.

Change your Perceptions and Understanding

Whatever the reasons for your stress it may not be necessary to experience it in the manner you might generally expect. One possibility is to initiate a shift in your thinking. Take appraisal, for example: you could see it as a terrifying and threatening experience or you could transform it into a welcome and challenging opportunity to demonstrate your strengths and highlight some areas for further professional development. I appreciate that this may be considerably easier said than done but remember that you are an able and conscientious professional and the appraisal operation has not been mounted to *catch you out* but rather to enhance teaching quality in general.

As suggested earlier in the chapter, it may be that you are feeling stressed because you are tired. Having a good sleep may help put everything back into perspective. Similarly chatting things through with a friend, rather than bottling them up, may put things into proportion again.

Your imagination can also play an important role in changing your perspective but, as indicated earlier, it may not be an appropriate strategy if you are prone to imaginative stress. Imagine what would happen, for example, if you did not complete your pile of paperwork tonight, tomorrow or even next week? You might irritate one or two people but, I suspect, nothing very serious — such as your world falling apart — would happen.

If you are inclined towards the stress of anticipation try to picture what is the very worst that could happen to you in this seemingly frightful situation which is about to happen. Would everyone start laughing at you? Unlikely. Would you have to be carried away kicking and screaming? Unlikely. Would your whole world fall apart? Unlikely. In other words, perhaps the power of the situation is not as great as you might imagine.

Another common suggestion is to imagine the other participants without any clothes on, but take care that your hilarity, lust or horror does not distract you too much from the matter in hand!

Changing your perceptions of a situation may also come about through your gaining greater insight of your emotions. Thus, having identified the cause, or causes, of your stress it is often helpful to examine what you are really feeling. It may be blindingly obvious — you have just broken your leg and you are in agony — in which case the rest of this paragraph will be of little relevance to you at the moment. Or it may be that the emotion at the forefront of your consciousness is not an accurate reflection of your true feelings. More specifically, in my experience, people often flare up or show other symptoms of anger when they find themselves in stressful situations. Almost invariably, however, they are masking other emotions such as fear, rejection and hurt. Next time you are angry try to unravel what you are really feeling. You may end up being frustrated and even angrier but, alternatively, you may discover that someone has really hurt you and, as a result, you are feeling rejected. With that knowledge perhaps you can handle the situation in a more constructive manner or cry rather than wanting to hit out and crack someone's jaw. Understanding your emotions can be an important step in tackling your stress.

Tackle the Situation

Facing up to and tackling the situation could be described as the 'grown up and sensible' way to cope with stress. It may not necessarily be the smart thing to do (would you fight when face to face with an angry bull?) nor, indeed, may it be worth the effort. For example, do you really need to expend considerable energy and possibly create great hurt by telling a retiring headteacher exactly what you think of him/her on the last day of term?

To tackle a stressful situation effectively for — as far as possible — all concerned you need to understand what exactly is the source of your stress, your perceptions and the possible options: sometimes this is straightforward. When Martin is under pressure at school he believes, 'The best way to deal with stress is to do the work.' If you are feeling hot and bothered, open a window.

Sometimes you may need help to unravel what is going on and how you feel about it. I cannot overemphasize the value of talking the situation through. You may find talking it over in your head is sufficient, or writing a diary; a colleague or close friend might help or — if you wish to ensure confidentiality and experienced guidance — you might find a professional counsellor, doctor or priest more helpful. It may be that you make the wrong choice of confidante initially but do not abandon the idea, rather seek out someone else to whom you relate more appropriately. Should you seek professional advice do not let other people's reactions influence you: no one need know that you are in therapy. Indeed there may be a free service — as there is in Norwich — so even your bank manager need never find out! (The best ways to root out such facilities in your area would be to contact your doctor, ask the Citizens Advice Bureau or Samaritans or look under 'Therapists' in the Yellow Pages.)

Talking things through might enable you to 'let go' of the stress. This can often happen if, for example, you feel hard done by: carrying the weight of resentment and ill-feeling can be a heavy and, possibly, soul-destroying burden. Talking might also involve addressing the 'object' of stress directly. This can often resolve the problem. For example, I used to find it irritating when every time I went to the biscuit tin it was empty. The family talked it over. Now, whenever someone notices that the stock is becoming dangerously low, they make a note on the perpetual shopping list which is always kept in the kitchen drawer.

If the problem is not so easily resolved, bringing it out into the open may at least make you feel better. No changes were made when Kate spoke to her headteacher about the school's system for break duties but, at least, the situation had been aired and Kate felt better as a result. Similarly Brenda apparently found it very therapeutic talking to me about her final teaching practice: the concept still 'terrified' her but she actually sought me out to say how much calmer she felt having voiced her anxieties.

Tackling the situation may mean adopting variations of the strategies described above. Thus, if you are feeling overloaded, acknowledge your needs and tactfully say 'No' to the next request for assistance, if necessary delegate (to a child, parent or partner) and even ignore some of the tasks you originally intended completing yesterday. The art, of course, is not so much in finding solutions here and now but in applying them when the chips are down and the heat is on. Easier said than done but then no one said it was necessarily simple!

Summary

A wide range of ideas and suggestions has been considered in this chapter. Some of them will be revisited later in the book but, in the meantime, a few key points might prove a helpful reminder:

Types of Stress

- Here and now stress
- Stress of anticipation
- Imaginative stress
- Reactive stress
- Chronic stress

Unravel your Stress

- Reduce the odds
- Ignore it
- Avoid it
- Remove yourself from it
- Acknowledge your needs and anticipate
- Compartmentalize
- Acknowledge and live with the situation
- Reduce the physical sensations
- Change your perceptions and understanding
- Tackle the situation
- A combination of these!

A Challenge

Consider one or two aspects of your life which you find irksome. Review the stress strategies described, reflecting on which (if any!) might alleviate the situation and try them. It is unlikely to make the situation worse and it could make it markedly better.

Further Reading

Both these books are comprehensive, and comprehensible, guides to the problems of stress and how best to deal with them:

Fontana, D. (1989) *Managing Stress*, London, The British Psychological Society in association with Routledge.
Kirsta, A. (1986) *The Book of Stress Survival*, London, Unwin Paperbacks.

More specialist issues which are covered in an accessible manner are dealt with in the following books:

DICKSON, A. and HENRIQUES, N. (1994) *Hysterectomy: The Woman's View*, London, Quartet Books.

DICKSON, A. and HENRIQUES, N. (1995) *Menopause: The Woman's View*, London, Quartet Books.

HUTCHINSON, B. (1994) 'Teachers' models of change and proposals for educational reform', *Cambridge Journal of Education*, **19**, pp.153–62.

LINDENFIELD, G. (1986) *Assert Yourself*, Wellingborough, Thorsens Publishers Limited.

SMYTH, A. (1990) *SAD: Seasonal Affective Disorder*, London, Unwin Paperbacks.

SECTION II
Challenges in Teaching

The following six chapters focus on different aspects of primary teachers' professional lives which often seem to prove particularly stressful. Much of the material arises from conversations I have had with practitioners at various stages of their careers — from diffident students to highly experienced headteachers. At first sight it might appear that some of the chapters are aimed at specific groups of individuals (e.g., beginning teachers) but I hope you will withhold judgment for the intention is that, with better understanding of their colleagues' stresses, people can help one another and work more effectively as a team.

2   Starting Out

Introduction

Whether you are an experienced teacher or new to the profession, starting a new job is often an exhilarating, challenging and daunting experience all rolled into one. Occasionally it can be a disaster. Occasionally it can be virtually problem-free. But, most often, people seem to fluctuate between highs and wobbles, uncertainties and pleasures, tiredness and exhaustion.

This chapter is intended for all in the teaching profession whether you are a 60-year-old headteacher who has been in the same school for the past thirty years or a 22-year-old straight out of college. Indeed it is particularly intended for the former and other colleagues who have been in the same school for a number of years. You are in a privileged position and, with your help and understanding, a new member of staff's first term can be made considerably easier and more pleasant. When the relationship between a beginning and experienced teacher works well both have much to gain. When it fails much — possibly irrevocable — damage can result. For success to ensue both parties need to offer support and understanding.

Your first impression may be that this chapter has been written primarily for those embarking on their first job. Certainly much of the chapter is of direct relevance to them and one of the intentions is that they should be able to identify with the contents and, as a consequence, feel less isolated. However, more experienced teachers starting a new job should also find this chapter informative and a useful reminder of some of the issues to consider when taking up a new post.

Much of the material came from ex-students of mine who have recently taken up teaching posts in the area but, now and again, reference will be made to comments from older, more experienced staff. I have also thrown in one or two of my own observations for good measure! It is difficult to know where to start for I do not wish to introduce anxiety where there is none nor, indeed, do I wish to pretend that life is necessarily a breeze with few complications when one sets out in a new job. Different people experience different problems at different stages in their new, possibly very different, situations. For the sake of simplicity, I will begin by discussing issues which might arise before the children arrive at the start of term.

Before the Classroom Door

On hearing they have been offered a job most students are over the moon. It may be several days, weeks, months, or perhaps never that the realization of their future *responsibility* hits them. It is undoubtedly a highly responsible job but, as Jack — a beginning teacher — described, he felt 'in control'; he had survived the threat of passing or failing his training and he was about to earn considerably more than his student grant. Moreover, while he appreciated that many people would have expectations of him — staff, parents, governors, children and so on — he recognized that *he* was the one who was considered fit for the job; not the others who had been sitting round him at interview, but *him*.

Deciding to apply for a job is the first of thousands of *decisions*. Several of these will be considered later in the chapter but, before crossing the school threshold, stand back and try to picture your life in and beyond teaching for the coming months. In doing so, rather than being daunted by the forthcoming challenge, perhaps you can minimize some of the decision making and thought of the next few weeks by forward planning both for home and school. Thus you might decide to delay choosing what colour to paint your new bedroom or you could spend a day cooking and freezing in readiness for those evenings when you will be tired and in need of a good meal.

Forward planning in school can involve all manner of tasks most of which can be categorized in terms of colleagues, the curriculum, systems, and your classroom.

Colleagues

Getting to know your colleagues can prove invaluable for they can not only initiate you into the ways of your new school but they can share your joys and troubles in times of need. Neither 'old-timers' nor new-comers should assume that good working relationships are automatic-ally established with 'hello' and a friendly smile. It may take a little more but sometimes it may be less straightforward, there being at least two sides to every story — some of which are hidden and some of which are only too apparent. The moment Kate walked in the door of her new school all she heard about was the 'wonderful' Mrs D whom she had replaced. 'Mrs D did this,' 'Mrs D did that,' and so it went on. On the point of developing a hearty dislike for the wonderful Mrs D, Kate actually met the lady and was pleasantly surprised to discover that she was not superwoman but simply an elderly, rather mouse-like woman who had clearly dedicated her life to teaching.

Part of the reason for Kate hearing so much about Mrs D may well be explained by the following comments. The first is made by someone in his third year of teaching and the second by someone who has been in the profession for many years.

> People feel intimidated, I think, by new members of staff: how good they are going to be, whether they'll be doing better than everyone else.

> To be honest I think I am a little scared of newcomers. They learn so many up-to-date ideas in college and they always seem to know best. It's a pity really because, over the years, I think my colleagues and I have done a lot of trying and testing and have gradually evolved strategies that work.

Joanne, a very experienced teacher, puts it down to fear of the unknown:

> I remember I didn't sleep when I knew the head was going to retire. I kept thinking about the new head coming and wondering what it would be like and will I be able to cope.

On the one hand, Sarah, in her first year of teaching, found it very useful joining an experienced staff.

> I know there will be someone within the group who will be able to answer a question I have. If so-and-so keeps misbehaving and you want to know how to break her from doing it, or change her, or whatever it is, the staff are supportive and will offer me alternative strategies.

On the other hand, Sarah often perceives herself as being more stressed than her colleagues.

> They are all very experienced and I am very much at the learning phase of the teaching experience, and they know that if you

try this, this and this together they don't work whereas I haven't gone through that yet. I'm still on the learning curve: very low down on the learning curve.

Jane's initial encounters with her colleagues were very unhappy.

There was a time at this school when I just couldn't face turning the handle of the staffroom door.

She felt it was important to make the effort as she was only too aware of the possibility of seeming 'standoffish'. Gradually it became apparent that the staffroom atmosphere was totally unrelated to her; rather than being the cause of tension she was very much on the sidelines, it transpired that there was an ongoing feud between two members of staff. Jane was obviously relieved but nevertheless it took her a long time to get used to the sudden silences which sometimes descended as she entered the room whenever one of the central players was discussing the other. Fortunately, every now and again, Jane meets some of her old college friends and they freely discuss their trials and tribulations. She would rather discuss school matters with her own staff but at least, she says, she has a group of people off whom she can bounce ideas and concerns.

In brief, a little insight, diplomacy and concerted effort in getting to know your colleagues can ease the early days in a new school.

The Curriculum

Some may criticize the National Curriculum but one of its advantages must surely be the structure it provides for newcomers to the profession: rather than begin from scratch you have, at least, something from which to start.

Maggie was also slightly surprised to find that all the hours she had had to spend on the 'the dreaded file' at college actually put her at an advantage when she began work.

Everybody does their own planning here but I don't think I found it as hard as other members of staff for whom it was new because I was used to doing planning for teaching practice. I just really followed on doing the same sort of thing but not in quite the detail you do for daily plans obviously.

Stephen likes the more structured approach of his school.

> We plan by brainstorming a topic together and then ensuring
> that we've covered all the subject areas that need to be covered.
> Those general plans we have to share but then specific daily
> plans we do individually although we share individual activities
> that went well. It's a nice mix. If something is not working or
> you're stuck or don't know how to solve a difficult problem,
> you know the other person is there and in touch with what you
> are trying to do.

None of the newcomers I spoke to found planning a major problem, although Susan said with feeling, 'It's not like teaching practice:
you have got to pace yourself.' She, it transpired, had considerably
overplanned and both she and her pupils had been exhausted by week
3, let alone half-term! Unlike Susan, remember that it is all right to ditch
some of your plans if the pace is too great or if, for some reason, your
activities are not working as well as you had hoped. Your efforts will not
be wasted as you may be able to use the lessons another time. More
importantly you will not have wasted your pupils' time and your patience trying to race your way through something less than appropriate.

Overambitious planning can also include insufficient attention being
paid to your role in the proceedings: you may have planned beautifully
for the children, providing them with a wide range of stimulating experiences but forgetting that all of the tasks for all of the pupils require
all of your attention all of the time!

In most cases the newcomers found some sort of school plan or
structure which acted as a useful support. Frequently this included joint
planning sessions with other teachers in the same year group. The
precise way the newcomer delivered the curriculum was generally left
up to them but, now and again, there were clashes in philosophy
which, perhaps in some cases, could have been avoided had the issue
been more fully discussed at interview. For example, Tom, after numerous applications, was delighted when he eventually gained a teaching
post in a more deprived area of a large city. He looked forward to using
lots of games and investigations in his teaching only to find that the
headteacher was most anxious that he follow the commercial schemes
used by the school and, if a child required extra help, to devise an
appropriate worksheet. Tom lasted a year and then went in search of
a job which was more in sympathy with his philosophy of education.
He found he could employ the worksheet philosophy but, throughout
that first year, he felt he was constantly having to bite his tongue and

hold his fire waiting until his second appointment when he could really try out his more progressive ideas.

A similarly difficult situation arose in Sam's school when a new headteacher arrived.

> Our new head has brought planning sheets that I disagree with quite strongly in that they're topic-based and they ask for a list under subjects, levels, attainment targets. They need to be filled in in the A, B or C under each of the attainment targets and the specific activities that you're doing with that topic. And I argued that the activities that you do should be open-ended and shouldn't be specifically targeted to a particular level or particular attainment target and that the levels relate to the children's performance and not to what you're planning. So you know that particular form has caused my blood pressure to go up once or twice.

To summarize, forward planning is certainly a good idea and should ease some of the pressures of the first few weeks but, remember, sticking rigidly to your plans can have quite the opposite effect!

Systems

As a newcomer to any organization there are various systems you have to assimilate. Some of these you will be told about when you arrive but some you will be left to discover for yourself, often because they are already so much a part of the school's routine that colleagues overlooked telling you about them. Some matter, some less so. As an experienced member of a team the more you can do to inform your new colleague of the school's systems the easier and safer it will be for them and their pupils.

One of the first and most important things to learn about is how the coffee is managed! To a small degree this is said in jest, but — if you are not already aware of it — most of you will very quickly come to appreciate how crucial it is to have a mid-morning break. It is many years since I have come across a staffroom where everyone has their own special chair but it is not uncommon for everyone to have their own mug and even, in a few cases, their own jar of coffee. It is as well to check. People will be only too happy to tell you and, if there are no such systems, they will almost invariably rather smugly tell you, 'Oh no, we're not one of those staffrooms where everyone has their own cup and special chair.' Check also who, how and when you should pay for any teas or coffees you have and whether this covers any biscuits which might appear from time to time. As Ulla says of staffrooms, 'They've all got their own idiosyncrasies really, haven't they?'

Before term starts there are several fundamental systems you should ascertain if at all possible. Firstly, what is the procedure in the event of a fire or any other life-threatening event? You, after all, will be responsible for your class: how should you respond to an emergency? Secondly, you should discover the system for meeting the children in the morning and sending them home in the afternoon. Sadly, more than ever before, you need to know who is allowed to pick up which child, ensuring that a stranger or absent parent does not persuade you that he or she has been given permission to do so. If you do not know the school's strategy for taking responsibility for the children in the morning and after school then *ask*.

A third, related, issue is what is the routine for dealing with parents especially if they have a complaint? Nell found the whole issue of parents quite tricky to start with.

> You often end up counselling parents down here. I find that quite difficult. Typically the ones one seems to encounter are the aggressive ones. And particularly last year when I wasn't fully aware of what the routine was and what procedures were for certain situations. I'm finding that much easier this year because I'm more aware of what the routines are and what the school's collective thinking on certain issues is. And therefore I'm more confident about what I'm saying to the parents. I don't think I could have learnt this at college because it seems to be so dependent on the school's ethos.

Fourthly, it is important that you find out what you should do if a child in your care has an accident. The response to this will, in part, depend on the law and, in part, on school policy. You may, for example, be held liable if you blunder in and do the wrong thing. Minor injuries — cut knees, knocks and bruises — are often dealt with by a welfare assistant and these, along with more serious accidents, will almost invariably be recorded in the school's accident book.

A fifth system which it is helpful to explore is whether the school has a whole school policy on discipline (it should) and what are the philosophy and procedures behind it. For example, are pupils encouraged to take responsibility for their own actions? Is 'talking things through' encouraged? Is it appropriate to send a child to another teacher if they are misbehaving? In time you will discover whether the policy preached and practised are one and the same thing but, in the mean-time, it is as well to see what procedures are formally recommended.

Resources are a sixth issue which you should consider prior to the start of term. Often the system is straightforward but nevertheless you should check where stocks of paper, pencils, exercise books etc., are kept; how many people share these items? (e.g., do you have your own personal supply of stationery or do the staff share everything?); how long the stock is expected to last (a term? a year?), and; what is the procedure when supplies are running low (e.g., 'It's too bad', 'You fill in a request', 'Mrs Y organizes that.')

Quite often equipment — especially if it is expensive — is shared between several members of staff which may make economic sense but, as Sam explains,

> The storage of stuff in school is quite a stressful thing. A lot of the materials are kept centrally and then, of course, it is always unpredictable who's got what. You know, if I need the globe and then somebody else wants to have it, then you're chasing around and it's a big school to get around . . . It's okay if you know exactly what you are going to need beforehand — al-though it's a first come, first served system — as people will generally let you have what you want, but it's difficult to do it on the spur of the moment, you know, if suddenly, if a child says to you something about the world and you think, 'I'll show them the globe'. It's not always easy to get one — to respond the same day.

'Resources' may often include human resources. Find out, for ex-ample, if and when you can hope for welfare help and whether it is customary to invite parents in to help in the classroom. Both can be of invaluable assistance but it is important that you recognize their assets and their limitations. All too often I have seen parent helpers idly sitting through sessions when a student has been talking to the class. This, not surprisingly, may be seen as a waste of their time and may result in a rapid decrease in volunteers. Fortunately, I have also seen assistants really complementing teachers: they do not replace the teacher but their talents, for example, may well raise the standard of art and craft in the classroom.

When discussing parental help you would also be wise to check with your colleagues whether there are any parents you perhaps should not welcome with open arms. Fortunately Tony was warned that Mrs W was prone to 'shouting and swearing at her kids' and so, rather than generally invite volunteers, he asked specific parents to help him. As it happens Mrs W did come forward and offer her services later in the term but Tony was able to say, 'Thanks but we're okay at the moment. If something comes up next half-term I'll ask you to come in.' He then made sure that he would not require further help for the remainder of the term!

You should also consider how you feel about having another adult in the room with you. Sheila said, 'It's almost as if it's an invasion if people come in.' Accordingly she often gives helpers tasks to do outside of the classroom such as, 'Could you just take this group and have a look at the trees.' Now and again other adults do work alongside her but she tries to select activities about which she is confident and remind herself that the other adults will have more than enough to do than attend to her!

As you will discover, schools all have their unique systems and routines. You should certainly explore those mentioned above in the early days of your appointment. You should also ask what general school duties you will be expected to cover and when. You will almost certainly be expected to do playground duty once a week but what about other responsibilities both within school hours and after the children have gone home? As an accomplished musician, for example, will you be expected to take on the recorder group?

A final issue you should consider, which is not exactly a system but which could prove invaluable, is to find out a little about the children's previous experience. Jenny, for example, found it helpful to know that her future class of 7 year olds had just left a rather traditional teacher who tended to favour whole class teaching. Accordingly Jenny amended her original plans and, rather than rushing in with a fully integrated day, she gradually introduced the notion of working in groups and following a more progressive routine. Again, therefore, a little advanced investigation into the school's systems and routines can save time and hassle once term starts.

Your Classroom

Spend as much time as you can getting to know your classroom before your pupils arrive. If you know where everything is then you are far more likely to feel confident and able to respond to the children's requests of where this, that and the next thing is located.

Ideally you will have time to arrange everything to suit your predicted needs (you are bound to want to make changes). If you do, you will need to address issues such as how independent do you wish your pupils to be. To save your own time and energy I would encourage you to have as much as possible clearly labelled and readily accessible at child height, bearing in mind safety issues (where will the scissors and glue go?), 'flickability' and related concerns: in other words, if at all possible, avoid having children sitting next to open shelves with interesting, easily movable items on them!

Check out any games, play equipment and books which might provide appropriate activities for the children when they have finished their assigned tasks and you are otherwise engaged.

Try to picture the children arriving at school on their first morning (see Figure 2.1). Will they know where to hang their coats or are you going to opt for free choice? What will be their impression of the classroom? (A few colourful, topic-related posters might be a good idea.) Will they know where to sit, put their bits and pieces, etc.? Will there be enough in the way of basic materials available for that very first day? For example, have you sharpened enough pencils, collected enough exercise books with one or two to spare in the event of unexpected additions to the class and so on? In other words, I suggest you work systematically through the day trying to predict your and the children's every need and *write* everything down rather than trying to commit it to memory and rushing around at the last minute. Julie admitted,

> I hadn't really much of a clue how to prepare my classroom but I chatted to one or two of the most recently qualified members of staff and they gave me some good ideas such as 'keep it simple, straightforward and attractive'. They also reminded me not to panic but to improvise or send a child to them to ask for help if I got stuck.

Jane, an experienced teacher, advises,

> In teaching you *must* come in before and get your room ready and think about what you are going to do. And that reminds me, *never* arrive at 9 o'clock when you teach because the rest of your day will be up the wall.

Early Days

The title to this section refers to your initial days as a fully qualified practising teacher and the fact that, day in, day out, you will be expected to be up with the lark: easy for some perhaps but considerably

Figure 2.1: Try to picture the children arriving at school on their first morning

harder for others! Most primary headteachers are only too aware of when individual members of staff arrive and, I can assure you, you do yourself no favours if you rush in at the last minute. In the vast majority of schools, arriving after 8.30am for a nine o'clock start is taken as a serious lack of commitment. It also makes it very hard to be on your best form and ready for the children's arrival.

Related to this early rising is the fact that, at the end of each and every day, you will be shattered! Teaching and an active social life every night of the week simply do not mix. That is not to say you should see yourself as a hermit from here on in. On the contrary, that would be rash and counterproductive, as you will see. Rather you need to recognize that early nights during the week are likely to become the rule rather than the exception. Martin, who is in his third year of teaching, explained, 'I'm only 30 but a lot of nights I end up in bed by half past eight'. He — as were the other beginning teachers I spoke to — was quick to add, however, that it was crucial to make full use of your leisure time. This theme will be discussed towards the end of this chapter and then again in Section III.

It is also important to recognize and accept that you are likely to catch every bug and germ that is going in the early months of your teaching career. As will be discussed in Chapter 6, the dilemma may often be whether you take a day off school in the hope you'll recover more quickly or whether you should soldier on.

When I asked my postgraduate students what they were most anxious about as they were about to embark on their teaching career, almost without exception they said '*control and discipline*'. Interestingly none of the many experienced teachers I spoke to saw it as a major issue. It may have been because they did not wish to tell me that they had frightful classroom control! Alternatively — and my observations suggest that this is more likely — they really found that, after an initial settling down period with every class at the beginning of the academic year, they had few discipline problems. This issue will be taken up again in Chapter 3 but, before moving on, whether you are starting out or changing schools, some of the following observations may prove reassuring.

The first is that if you look and feel the part of a professional teacher then the chances are that you will have fewer discipline problems. Right from the start of their training some of my students have an air of confidence which suggests that they expect their pupils to behave and, indeed, in most cases they do. In part it helps if you have had experience with children before as a parent, volunteer or in a previous job. Maria certainly found this to be the case.

I thought it was helpful having had a family. I think you have a much more realistic view of children and you know they're not always going to be good and sometimes they're going to be naughty. And you can be cross with them and they will understand that they have done something that made you cross . . . I don't mean that you should be thunder and lightning all the time but I do think it's healthy for children to understand that they've overstepped the mark and that they've upset you . . . When I worked for social services I quite often had people who wanted to become teachers and an awful lot of them had terrible problems with actually saying 'no' to children . . . And because they were wanting to be friends with the children they felt if they said 'no' the children wouldn't like them any more. If you have had your own children I think you can say 'no' with a different sort of confidence and know it will be okay.

The second observation is that you will not be alone if you experience discipline problems. Roy remembers,

In the first class I had there were two severely disruptive children and last year there was one: the emotional personal stress of dealing with him all the time was exhausting.

Part of the problem, he explains, was that,

Coping with Gary definitely detracted from teaching the rest of the class. It became a matter of conscience: feeling distracted not giving what you know you could to the rest of the class.

Roy's problem did not just go away but, through talking with colleagues, reading (see the end of the chapter), observations and trial and error, he devised strategies which seemed to work for him and his class.

And finally Martin, an excellent teacher, explains how he adapted a certain tolerance and coping strategy for his first two-year post which, unconsciously, he modified in his second job.

At my first school, children seemed to be shouting out or crawling under the table all the time. But because it was happening all the time you didn't notice it . . . I guess I was in a constant state of stress, if you like, or hyperactivity . . . To be honest I found the children quite easy to handle there but, recently, having been in this school for a year, it was quite a shock to me how I'd — not lost my touch — but forgotten what it was like . . . It happened the other day with one lad from another class who was put into my class. He started misbehaving and my heartbeat went up and suddenly I lost where I was and it took a few seconds to sort of come back round again and think, 'Right, what were we up to and where were we going'. I think it throws things out of joint not just for the teachers but I'm sure for the children as well . . . It worried me a little to think, 'Oh well, I've lost that ability to discipline a little.' But then I thought about it the next day and I thought, 'Oh no, I can handle that still.' It's just a case of what you're used to, I suppose.

In other words, on the basis of previous experience (in your case it might be teaching practice or an earlier job), Martin knew that he could manage a demanding class but he needed to remind himself of this fact, having increased his expectations of pupil behaviour and — to some extent — decreased his vigilance. In brief, you will not be alone if you have discipline problems but, as will be discussed more fully in Chapter 3, you would be wise to stay calm, observe, talk about it with colleagues, read and remember successful strategies that you, or someone else, have tried in the past.

Concerns over *academic content* was another issue about which beginning teachers said they sometimes worried. Some admitted that, now and again, they were not entirely sure whether they understood what they had to teach but they were too afraid to ask. Simon explained,

I think subject knowledge is going to be a bit of a problem for me in the future because my grammar is awful. I'm going to get myself a simple book of English grammar.

I often suggest to students that they buy a 'Noddy' (i.e., an extremely basic) book for subjects which cause them some anxiety. It is the responsible thing to do rather than blundering through something you — and, consequently, almost certainly your pupils — do not understand. Listed at the end of this chapter are such books that our primary students found helpful. Teachers' handbooks can also prove surprisingly helpful. If you cannot find an appropriate book there are two main options: either you avoid the topic altogether (not a good idea if it is a crucial part of the curriculum) or you pluck up your courage and ask someone about it. The latter may be awkward but (a) surely it is infinitely more responsible than misleading children and (b) you may well find that the person you ask is also a little unclear! Headteacher, Jane, has a very open approach, 'If I don't know it, I say it. It doesn't worry me!'

An associated issue is knowing at what level to pitch the work and how to progress through it in appropriate stages. This is particularly difficult in your first year of teaching an age group. Reassuringly, by her second year of teaching Jane was able to say, '. . . now I know roughly where they should be'. Five suggestions which might be of help:

1   Ask the children's previous teacher if you might go through his/her records of work and discuss an appropriate starting point.

2   If applicable, ask teachers of parallel classes how they generally begin the year.

3   Start the term with a series of open-ended tasks which will give you an idea of what you might reasonably expect from the children. These might include their drawing a picture, writing about themselves or asking them to design an object which moves or inviting them to explore a scientific concept such as why inflated balloons generally go up but empty ones go down. As with any approach, these tasks should be accompanied by observation on your part followed by discussions with the children. I appreciate that neither is easy when you have a class of not one but thirty children but, if you are prepared to take days rather than hours and if you follow the other suggestions, it will be time well invested.

4   Remember the National Curriculum! Sarah found, '. . . it's been more of a stress reliever because it shows you the levels and what the children should be doing'.

5   Follow your professional instincts if at all possible. This may mean you jumping on a faster or slower escalator than suggested by the National Curriculum or your colleagues. Maria, for example, found herself in a real dilemma when her colleagues decided that France would be the topic for the term: her pupils did not even know that they lived in a city called Norwich, let alone in a country called England. She opted for a more gradual approach than her colleagues. This, in itself, increased her stress but, I suspect, less so than having a class full of bored children who were totally out of their depth.

A final reassuring comment on this issue from Jane,

> They do learn, no matter what. They're like sponges so no matter what's going on around them they absorb it. So long as you've got the right climate in your classroom they learn.

I am not, of course, suggesting that you sit back and relax but, as I will discuss below, I am advocating a realistic approach.

Sarah finds an added strain when preparing children for their next school.

> I think there's more pressure on you to conform to the National Curriculum and to get through a certain amount. The pressure is really on to get them as good as you possibly can.

Martin admits,

> You're concerned, although you shouldn't be, with what you haven't done rather than with what you have.

He goes on,

> So you kind of make yourself think — even if a child has done just one piece of writing this week — 'That's a really good piece of work'. You know they've been doing other things even if you haven't got something written down. You know they've done some painting or that they've been negotiating with their friends. You feel under pressure but it's just the classic problem, there is just not enough time.

With this in mind, do your best and remember that processes, as well as products, are a crucial part of the National Curriculum: you may not be able to produce tangible evidence but your pupils may have achieved something far more valuable than a completed piece of paper.

Paperwork is another facet of your job which you may feel is never-ending and impossible to complete. If you have recently qualified you probably will not find it such a problem as some of your more experienced colleagues who began their careers when very few records were required. Amazing as it may seem, those dreaded teaching practice files should have got you well practised in paperwork. This issue will be discussed in more detail in Chapter 3 but, in the meantime, remember the importance of keeping your records up to date, otherwise report writing may prove to be an impossible nightmare. And remember that it is not a competition: some of your colleagues may take no time at all while others may be more like Susie.

> I take a long time to think. I mean, some people can write things out really quickly and think really quickly but it takes me a long time to think.

Discussion

In my discussion with beginning teachers I asked what advice they would give to people starting out on their career. There was never any hesitation in their suggestions and, indeed, some had several tips which, I suspect, we should all take on board in our professional lives.

It is important to be realistic and kind to yourself. Sarah advises,

> Take it easy in the first year. Do not throw yourself in too much. Initially do not go overboard trying to do everything in the first year but try to build up to things. Try to set your sights within range and remember that it is not going to be like one long teaching practice.

When I asked her whether she would have followed her own advice she laughed and said, 'Probably not because I was very keen and highly motivated.' I suspect that applies to most of you reading this book but nevertheless her suggestion is valid especially if you have moved to a new part of the country or find yourself in an unfamiliar school environment. In both cases both you and the children will take that little bit longer to get to know and understand one another. Moreover you may find yourself a bit deskilled. This will be discussed more in the chapter on change (Chapter 7), but basically it means that as you concentrate on acquiring new skills your performance in familiar tasks might not be of its usual high standard.

Whether you like it or not, you will not be able to do everything you would like to and Sam stresses the need to prioritize and 'not to worry about it'. Martin advises,

> Take your breaks. When it comes to break time, take it. When it comes to lunch time — even if it's only half an hour — take it. If somebody says, 'Look, I'll take your class for storytime this afternoon,' say, 'Okay, fine, take it.' I used to be, 'Oh no, I'll have them,' as if proving to myself, 'I can do this,' but now I don't feel guilty. If a break is offered to you, take it.

The teachers also advised an objective and constructive approach to criticism. People are bound to observe you in your first year and, for the most part, I hope you find their feedback realistic and informative. Some are not so lucky: Maria was less than impressed when an adviser came to observe her but rather than be demoralized by his criticisms she reflected,

He wasn't very aware of what goes on in first schools. He's not a first school person. He was saying things that sounded like anathema to first schools, like there was too much going on in the classroom. I don't think he had any understanding of how often children need to change activities because their concentration span isn't long enough to be spending all day doing one thing for the most part.

Maria was not trying to excuse her part in what the adviser considered to be a weak performance. Rather she was confident of her own philosophy and abilities and had 'very supportive' colleagues. Sheila stresses the need to try 'to see the positive in yourself and all the good things that you do. It's rather difficult but I find it invaluable when I've had a rough day.'

As a teacher trainer I am very keen that practitioners constantly reflect on their own practice for it seems a vital form of professional development. Indeed, those who evaluate most constructively tend to make the best teachers. It can often be useful to extend your reflection and discuss issues over with colleagues. Sally found 'the head very approachable . . . Right from the start she's supported me and has encouraged me to discuss problems with either her or the teacher of the parallel class.'

Mandy was more suspicious of her headteacher.

A headteacher could, in theory, perform the role of a mentor if you didn't have this worry of forever trying to impress all the time. I'm sure that if I went to my head and said, 'I've got a problem,' she'd help me. But you don't ever want to admit it.

She was, however, fortunate in finding an adviser whom she could trust.

She was always very positive and always made you see your strengths. She's somebody that you need to have at the end of every week to say to you, 'Look, you've done this this week and wasn't it really good'.

Mandy also meets up with old college friends from time to time — 'It's comforting to talk to friends' — but she adds, 'It's almost as if you need somebody who's more experienced to talk to, somebody who's been there before.'

Sally agrees that it is a good idea to meet up with other people new to the profession,

> We either sort of prop each other up or find we're all in the same boat. Both can be very good.

An added advantage to these meetings, Sally feels, is that they are enjoyable social occasions. These, she believes, are all part of 'making time for yourself' which, she argues, is crucial.

> I do yoga on a Monday night and the family knows that's what happens. I also make a point of going out about once a fortnight and I try to do my lace as often as I can. I am doing a very complicated piece at the moment and I have to concentrate on it totally. I find it very relaxing.

Martin endorses the view of making time for yourself. Initially he found that he 'almost ran myself into the ground' but, with experience, he has learnt to say to himself, 'No, it's time to stop now'. He now does quite a bit of cooking at home.

> I'm not a very good cook but I guess what it is, is something for yourself. I listen to music and I guess it's kind of starting to think about yourself again.

And, finally, Sally advises,

> Stick with it. The second year of teaching is completely different from the first and much easier.

Summary

Everyone can play an important role in welcoming and supporting new members of staff.
- Teaching is a responsible job and *you* were the one they appointed.
- Keep less urgent decision making to a minimum in the early days.
- Do as much forward planning as possible:

- ◆ get to know, use and understand your colleagues;
- ◆ prepare the curriculum but be ready to abandon unsuitable plans;
- ◆ endeavour to become familiar with the school's systems (e.g., coffee), safety and accident procedures, handling parents, discipline, material and human resources;
- ◆ discover the teaching methods of your pupils' previous teacher;
- ◆ arrange your classroom to welcome the children and meet your philosophy;
- ◆ list all the jobs you have to do rather than commit them to memory and panic.
- You are likely to be tired and more prone to illness.
- You may have control and discipline problems but:
  - ◆ try to look and feel professional;
  - ◆ remember you are not alone;
  - ◆ read, observe and talk to colleagues;
  - ◆ remind yourself of earlier successes.
- If academic content poses a problem read a 'Noddy' book on the subject, refer to teachers' handbooks or be brave and ask a colleague.
- Use the National Curriculum, colleagues, open-ended tasks, observation, discussion and reflection to gauge the appropriate level of curriculum content for your pupils. And remember to follow your professional instincts on the matter!
- Remember, when it comes to learning, 'They're like sponges'.
- Curriculum coverage can be a pressure but take heed; processes as well as products are important.
- Paperwork is never-ending but try to keep up to date and remember it is not a competition to see who can finish it first!
- Be realistic in your goals.
- Deskilling may occur particularly if you find yourself in an unfamiliar environment.
- Prioritize.
- Take your breaks and offers of help.
- Try to handle criticism constructively.
- Ask for advice and feedback from people you respect and trust. These may be your headteacher, colleagues, local education advisers or friends from college days.
- Take time for yourself.
- Stick with it!

Further Reading

There seem to be surprisingly few good books on the early years of teaching but there are several which focus on specific aspects of professional practice which could prove useful. Some of these are listed at the end of Chapter 3. In addition, books which my students have found helpful on the subject of *discipline* are:

BASSEY, M. (1978) *Practical Organisation in the Primary School*, London, Ward Lock Educational.
COHEN, L. and COHEN, A. (eds) (1987) *Disruptive Behaviour*, London, Harper and Row.
DAVIS, R. (1988) *Learning to Teach in the Primary School*, Sevenoaks, Hodder and Stoughton.
DOCKING, J.W. (1987) *Control and Discipline in Schools*, London, Harper and Row.
FONTANA, D. (1985) *Classroom Control*, London, Methuen.
MCMANUS, M. (1989) *Troublesome Behaviour in the Classroom*, New York, Routledge.
ROBERTSON, J. (1981) *Effective Classroom Control*, Sevenoaks, Hodder and Stoughton.
ROGERS, B. (1990) *You Know the Fair Rule*, Harlow, Longman.

Students also recommend the following 'Noddy' books which focus on specific subjects:

BARNES, R. (1987) *Teaching Art to Young Children*, London, Allen and Unwin.
BARNES, R. (1993) *Art, Design and Topic Work, 8–13*, London, Routledge.
GOWER, R. (1990) *Religious Education at the Primary Stage*, Oxford, Lion.
HARLEN, W. and JELLY, S. (1989) *Developing Science in the Primary Classroom*, London, Oliver and Boyd.
HAYLOCK, D.W. and COCKBURN, A.D. (1989) *Understanding Early Years Mathematics*, London, Paul Chapman.
SHERRINGTON, R. (ed.) (1993) *The ASE Primary Science Teachers' Handbook*, Hemel Hempstead, Simon and Schuster Education.
THYER, D. and MAGGS, J. (1991) *Teaching Mathematics to Young Children*, London, Cassell.
WETTON, P. (1988) *Physical Education in the Nursery and Infant School*, London, Croom Helm.

3   Classroom Stresses

Classrooms and, even more so, the pupils inside them lie at the very heart of school teaching. It is not surprising that they sometimes prove to be rather stressful environments given that thirty individuals are shut in a room together for hours on end, day in, day out, with the vast majority of them having little or no choice in the matter. And yet it is the children that the teachers, almost without exception, said made the job worthwhile.

> The children are the best thing about the job.

> I love the children: they're such characters. I have so much fun in here.

> I really enjoy the response from the children. It's seeing them come as little individuals — sort of every which way — and it's drawing them together. I love to see them gel and become my children without knocking out their individuality. I find that a real challenge: that's a joy to me.

Volumes and volumes have been written about children and classrooms and it is not the role of this chapter to repeat that (although some useful references are listed at the end of the chapter) nor, indeed, is it to teach my grandmother to suck eggs. Rather the aim is to share with you some of the thoughts and anxieties experienced by some of the many teachers to whom I have spoken. Sometimes there may be answers, but not necessarily: at least knowing that someone else has had similar problems can be remarkably comforting.

'Smile Please'

One of the problems is that everyone seems to know about teaching and is only too ready to give you a piece of friendly advice the intention of which is to solve most, if not all, of your professional problems at a stroke. John Eggleston explains,

In modern society teachers have a problem with status. Because everybody has at one time been at school, most people believe that they themselves have some or even most of a teacher's expertise and capability ... Teachers lack the mystique that normally enhances professional status and power, and are subject to public attempts to control and constrain them: by legislation, public opinion and even, occasionally, by media ridicule and prejudice. (1992, p.2)

Sylvia, a teacher of 30 years' experience, says that one aspect of the above that she finds stressful is the fact that

You're dealing with people and, at the end of the day, your consumers are the pupils, the parents, the governors, visitors to the school. We're answerable to so many people, I think, with very high expectations of us.

Added to this are numerous assumptions, as Cynthia, a reception class teacher, explained:

It was some time ago now we had a visitor and my children were walking down the corridor in a long line and this lady looked at them and said, 'Aahh, look at them walking nicely,' and I thought, 'Good grief, she's no idea how difficult it was to get them like that.' And I was so proud of the way they were quietly walking. That was a real achievement and I suppose it looked quite natural and, really, I suppose that was how it should look, but an awful lot of groundwork went in first.

'Sometimes,' she added, 'parents say all sorts of funny old things to you and I'm left thinking, "Here am I busting a gut to care about the children."'

Marian cites an example which might have been echoed by most of the practitioners I spoke to:

It is stressful actually matching up what you believe the children should be doing in terms of your philosophy and perhaps what parents perceive as being the right thing. I mean one of my children came in — and we've virtually got rid of scheme maths in this school, thank goodness — and she came in with eight books all beautifully filled in and then Mum says to me, 'Oh, did Mary show you her maths books?' And I said, 'Yes, she did', and I didn't know whether to say, 'Oh well, you know, I'm just a little bit concerned about her filling in these maths books because it's really against what we believe in.' She's a mum who helps in the classroom and obviously they're doing it because they feel I'm not.

And, of course, while coping with all these criticisms and suggestions, you are expected to maintain your calm professional manner. Susie describes it graphically,

> There are a lot of teachers who say that at the end of a day at school you have to 'uncrease your mask' because you go around smiling all day.

Classrooms

Very often you have little or no say in which classroom you will have. Diane considers,

> I could do with a lot more space especially when we're modelling and all the group activities are going on, you feel you can't help but fall over each other and bits and pieces, however carefully you think you've organized it.

Sometimes the size of the room can radically affect the way you teach.

> I really want some creative work going on, such as art or clay or whatever, and to have some other tasks going on such as language or maths, but it's not fair on those children who are trying to concentrate to have somebody pounding away at clay or painting. It means I can't really get my integrated day in all the time.

Susan finds the location of her classroom very difficult to cope with.

> It's right at the end of the school and there's an entrance foyer before the other classrooms and I feel very isolated down there. The positive side is that it's spacious and the children can move, but it's very cold and uncomfortable and there's no cosy corner to sit and read in. It's just not cosy; it's just draughty and cold.

John and Justine are more fortunate in their assigned classrooms but, as they say, it is important to make the environment as pleasant as possible.

> One of the things I have often said is that, for a large part of the day, it's you and the children in the classroom and so you make it good and comfortable and bright and lively and stimulating for the children but, as it is also my environment, I do it for myself as well.

> To be honest the school is dirty. And I think that if I'm expecting children to produce work that looks nice they can't be working in a dirty area. Sometimes I get frustrated about it and I do clean the classroom myself from time to time.

On the subject of creating a conducive atmosphere, Julia adds,

> I'm really keen on having my children being independent and getting along and trying to avoid stresses for them as well: I think that helps me too so I don't ever shout or flare up. If I see trouble brewing, trying to deal with it straight away.

Bill Laar and his colleagues in their book, *Effective Teaching*, discuss how to bring about a good classroom environment but remind us,

> Such environmental richness is not easily created and administered without unremitting effort on behalf of the teacher. (1989, p.24)

Wouldn't it be nice if parents, visitors and even headteachers appreciated our efforts from time to time!

A crucial aspect of the environmental atmosphere is you and how you are portraying yourself. If you are relaxed and well-planned then life should be considerably easier for, as Bill Laar dramatically puts it, '. . . unsatisfactory teacher planning is the learner's nightmare' (1989, p.12). And, as we know, an uncomfortable learner can markedly increase your workload (see below). Val Rowland and Ken Birkett also recommend thorough preparation:

As with the practice of most career skills, success is propor-
tional to the effort you put into effective planning. (1992, p.62)

'That is all very well', you may say, 'but what about the time to do it
in?' Lack of time will be explored more fully in Chapter 6 but let us
focus on actual planning for the moment.

Most experienced teachers can improvise — Marie calls it 'door-
handle preparation' — but Sarah never likes to do it 'more than a few
minutes' and Rachel sighs, 'You seem to pay the price for it later if
you're not properly prepared or you don't do something you wanted
to do because you haven't got the materials together or you haven't
thought it through properly.'

Whole school or, alternatively, year group planning seems to be
the least stressful *providing* you work well with your colleagues and
can be fairly autonomous. 'That way', June explains, 'we share all the
ideas and the workload.' When you do not get on with your colleagues
or no one else is teaching the same year group, planning can be considerably harder and more time consuming. Yvonne recalls her early
years of teaching.

> To start with it was very hard because, although I had been
> used to planning at college, I began teaching Year 5 children
> and I had never taken that age before so it was like starting
> from scratch and there was no one to help me and very few
> resources in the school. Now it is much easier as I have built up
> a stock of ideas and resources but it still seems to take ages and
> I really envy teachers who can work together.

Working with others is not always as trouble-free as she imagines (see
Chapter 4). Wendy recounted,

> We were supposed to work as a team and I guess we tried but
> we could never agree so now we just work on our own. It saves
> a lot of tension and hassle.

Teachers who appeared to find preparation relatively stress-free
tended to use the structure of the National Curriculum and engage in
three types of planning, broadly speaking: long-term, weekly and daily
with visualization. Norma describes how she operates the first two of
these.

> There are three of us in my year group and we have a year
> group leader and we get together before the end of a term and

we just chat about what we're doing next. We've known in advance because we plan a year ahead for topics. And then over the holiday I usually do a rough plan and when we get back we have a big year group meeting where we work out the general topic web for the term . . . And then every week I usually work my topic out so that I think, 'Right, the first week I can do invasion, or whatever'. I try to make, in that weekly plan, a balance of activities really making sure that I have a little bit of everything.

Marianne and her colleagues seemed to combine the two approaches and include assessment.

We do our planning as a group fortnightly on a Thursday and then it's all done. We spend a couple of hours after school doing it. And within that we plan our assessment as well so we all know what we're doing over that fortnight.

Visualizing a day or a session appears to be particularly hard for students but Rose says it is crucial and she likes to, '. . . spend twenty minutes just thinking about my day and the sort of activities the children are going to do.' That way she minimizes the likelihood that the paint is not mixed, that there are insufficient of x, y or z or whatever, or that she has provided an inappropriate balance of activities such that three groups will need her simultaneously. She can also markedly reduce the possibility of Sammy or Sarah not knowing what to do because she has not given them sufficient information on how to proceed.

Planning ahead, of course, can never be foolproof for it omits to — and indeed cannot — fully take into consideration your pupils and their responses. And it is here, perhaps, that the real art and challenge of teaching lie.

Teaching

I really love my job but sometimes I don't know whether to laugh or cry when I explain something, ask a question and a child comes out with something totally unexpected in response. Like the other day I was talking about sharing 12 sweets between three friends and Tanya said that she would give Mary 6 because she liked her, Sally 2, Zoe none as she was on a diet and she'd keep 4 for herself!

As you might have guessed, Wendy was experiencing what might be described as 'the thinking child' syndrome. This is discussed in detail in the literature (see references at the end of this chapter) and it is what can make teaching a stimulating and exciting challenge or — depending on your mood and energy levels — a seemingly never-ending uphill struggle. It might not be so stressful if you only had one child to contend with but, as Norma says, 'You've got 25 or so little beings and they're yours for the year and the responsibility for their education is on your shoulders.'

Marianne finds that she gains a lot of information from watching her children work but is disturbed to observe,

> I'm not thinking about it as much as I should in terms of what the children are actually doing and where they might be going to next. I seem to have lost that a little bit. Perhaps because we have to focus on so many different things now. I think now we've got so much on our plates that you tend to flit a little bit . . . Added to which there seems to be such a large ability range in here it's incredible, and that's very stressful because you have to cover everybody.

Norma adopts a systematic approach to observation,

> I've got a card index file where I bring a card to the front and try to observe that child during the day so that I can note something down. Well I haven't done it for two or three days, although I've got it in my head. I know I must record those things tonight otherwise they've gone.

Rachel tends to,

> . . . jot down incidents that have happened during the day and then I write them up. I don't think I need to be as meticulous about it really but I think it helps my teaching and I use them for report writing obviously.

In passing, it is interesting to note that none of the teachers I spoke to reported that they found it stressful actually talking to their pupils — finding the time to do so created anxiety (see below and Chapter 6) — and yet, as these writers describe, it is a highly skilled activity:

> An experienced teacher will know the importance of the timing of their intervention in the learning process. Knowing when to

Figure 3.1: *Added to which there seems to be such a large ability range...*

explain, when to allow discovery, when to be involved, and when to stand aside is all part of the teacher's professional role. (Rowland and Birkett, 1992, p.47)

But one thing effective teachers have in common is the appreciation that the quality of intervention lies at the heart of the quality of the teacher's work in the classroom. (Laar, 1989, p.26)

I very much suspect that the quality of these interactions must decrease when one is under pressure but, equally, my observations suggest that professionalism ensures that teacher–pupil interactions are one of the last things to suffer when a practitioner is feeling stressed.

There can, however, be an ongoing stress if you have a wide range of ability in your class. As Tanya says, 'Split age ranges: that's quite a pressure.' Olive finds such classes a mixed blessing,

I can see both the benefits and the drawbacks by having a mixed Year 5 and Year 6 class because it means that some of my weaker Year 6 children don't feel as out on a limb as they would do otherwise. There are two or three who really can benefit from working with the Year 5 children. But for some of the very able children — I can think of three — it's difficult to actually stretch them enough and yet meet the needs of the younger ones.

Norma finds that the real pressure comes not so much from a wide age range but a very broad attainment range. In her Year 3 class she has several non-readers. That, in itself, she feels she could cope with but,

The children have been bad attenders so you do whatever you can when you see them and then they don't attend for a couple of weeks and it's almost as if you are back where you started from. And then I have a very bright child so I'm providing for that sort of spectrum and everybody else in between and making sure I give everybody equal attention and getting everything into the week. It's hard enough with assemblies out and remembering to read a story. The week's too short.

Such problems are intensified if one has what I euphemistically call a lively or demanding group of individuals in your class.

Control and Discipline

Lorna was very fed up when she told me,

> I had a lovely class before Christmas but since then I've had two very difficult new ones and it's amazing the difference those two children have made: incredible.

For, as Jean explains,

> It can be very stressful if things just tip over that balance where things are going well if you have a difficult or large class.

Part of the stress seems to arise from guilt and frustration.

> When a child is having a hard time at home you worry about them but it's not really personally stressful but it's frustrating because you know that they can't perform adequately if they're not secure and happy at home.

> I find it quite difficult when I plan to sit down and teach a particular point and, instead, I find myself actually having to sort out fights or stop someone flushing felt tips down the loo or something else that you feel you can't easily ignore.

> Having a disruptive child definitely distracts from teaching the rest of the class. It's a matter of conscience: feeling distracted and not giving what you know you could be to the rest of the class.

On the one hand, teachers of younger children seem to find discipline less of a problem than colleagues further up the school.

> I find in reception it's containable because they're that much smaller. As soon as it has appeared I've been able to stamp on it and it's been stopped straight away.

Brenda thinks the difference is a lot to do with having time to form relationships.

> It's all down to relationships with the children and as you move up the school you almost have to compromise that situation

because you never seem to have time to make a relationship with a child; you've just got to get them on to the next National Curriculum level.

On the other hand, Iona says that she and her early years colleagues often have a more taxing time than the teachers in the local middle school for,

> ... in a first school you take all and sundry. I had quite a few disturbed children last year and one in particular was a real problem. It got to the stage where I thought, 'If this is what teaching is today I don't want to go on much longer.' But now that he's gone to the middle school he's in a special unit. It's certainly about time but I wish they had done it far, far sooner.

Olive implicitly endorses the idea of earlier statementing.

> I find it stressful when I've got children in my class whose needs are really beyond what the ordinary classroom experience can offer in terms of emotional and social needs as well. It affects the lives of all the children and although, to some extent, you need to learn to accommodate to each other, there are limits to the amount of accommodation children should have to make, I think.

Part of the problem seems to be that many teachers have not been trained to cope with some of the more disturbed children one finds in some of today's classrooms and well-meant advice can create further problems.

> Last year it was stressful because I was told that with this difficult boy I'd got to try to ignore the naughty things and praise the good things. But then you see you've got the fairness business coming in and the other children can see you've ignored something and they think, 'Well, if he can get away with it, why can't I?' It's difficult to know how to balance something like that.

Fortunately for their sanity, several of the teachers I spoke to echoed Kate's thoughts.

> I found discipline a problem in the past but I don't now. I think the longer you teach and the longer you are working in a school

the less of a problem discipline becomes because of the strategies you develop.

Moreover experience helps you reduce your emotional involvement as Steven and Norma explain.

> You just have to tell yourself, 'Right, I'm not going to let this get to me. I'm not going to let a class of 5 year olds grate on me.'

> Because so many of them have problems I can't worry about them all. I do care for them but I know I can't give them all that they need so I just have to — to a certain extent — cut myself off and think, 'Right, let's have you leaving here reading, writing and knowing a basic bit of number and having had a little bit of fun.'

Having said that, one of the principal control strategies teachers adopted was getting to know and like their pupils.

> I think that once you've got that rapport and they know that you like them and they like you you can't really lose.

> Ultimately they're not going to want to displease you if you've got a good relationship with them.

> I think respect is a mutual thing. For the most part if you respect the children they'll respect you and if they don't at their age it isn't disrespect, it's not knowing how to behave appropriately or being used to something different in their home environment.

This last point, I think, is particularly pertinent for young children or those new to a school: children are often told what *not* to do but, unless teachers make a specific point of telling them, they may not be aware of what they actually are supposed to do.

Reviewing several studies, Carolyn Evertson and Alene Harris (1992) concluded that both academic and behavioural expectations need to be specifically planned and clearly defined for each new class: it is not so much how teachers stop misbehaviour but how they prevent problems in the first place which characterizes effective practitioners. Thus they observed that the best teachers began the year by:

- preparing and planning classroom rules and procedures in advance;

- communicating their expectations clearly;
- establishing routines and procedures, and teaching them along with expectations for appropriate performance;
- systematically monitoring student academic work and behavior; and
- providing feedback about academic performance and behavior. (1992, p.76)

Evertson and Harris also recognize that no management system can stop all misbehaviour but recommend adopting unobtrusive techniques such as physical proximity or eye contact to curb minor misdemeanours as, '. . . punishment neither teaches desirable behavior nor instills a desire to behave' (1992, p.76). Often a whole school policy can prove very helpful.

> We have a policy in this school of supporting each other if we have a difficult child and part of that policy is that if a child is being really difficult and the teacher can't cope then we send them to another teacher or, sometimes, the head.

Occasionally it can prove exceedingly difficult to calm a distraught child.

> If a child is really upset — like we had a child last year who was biting and kicking us because he was so distressed — the situation is very stressful. The problem is when a child has lost control and giving him or her that control back again without causing damage to anybody or anything.

Kate explained how she, as a headteacher, handled a particularly awkward situation.

> I had this child in my room, and he had had to be carried yelling and screaming to my room. He was desperately trying to get out of the door, and normally if I just sit by the door and carry on with some work the child just kind of blows it all out and calms down then you can talk with them. But this particular child, he proceeded to kick and bang and hit the door, and me. He was making real swipes for me. He started throwing things about the room and not just kind of gently tipping things up but actually with real force, actually throwing things so that things were hitting the window — a great box of Lego. The only thing

I could do to control him — because my initial reaction was, well let him throw a few things about and get it out of his system and he'll be OK, but it didn't stop, and for an hour he was in my room in an extremely disturbed state and I ended up having to hold his hands, physically restraining him, which I don't like to do to a child, because if I didn't he was going to hurt himself, or hurt me or damage things in the room. I've never been in that situation before. And when he'd finally calmed down and we'd read a book together and it was all resolved, I was really shaking. It was one of the most stressful situations I'd ever been in. He was in such a state and so strong that I couldn't even get out of my room to contact another member of staff or the secretary or anything, and it was awful. I think that was probably one of the most stressful situations I've ever experienced.

As a result of this experience Kate has revised her practice.

And since then I've been dealing with the same child. I didn't ever want to put him in that situation again or myself in that situation again, so they're having to manage him in different ways so if he gets into a state — he has a tendency to run off, you see, but we found that if we let him run, the last thing you should do anyway is run after a child, you just watch where he is — he usually comes back in and calms down. So we've had to look at other ways of dealing with him. So if he gets distressed now I try and actually cope with him not in my room but in the classroom situation or slightly away from it but not both of us confined. So once again it's kind of the relationships thing . . .

Despite your hard work sometimes you may have to accept that your strategies will not always work, probably through no fault of your own.

This afternoon there were two groups of children arguing about a particular toy they wanted to play with and they were dealing with it badly and that really upset me as I felt let down and disappointed in some way.

I've got a couple of parents who are really up in arms about a little girl in our class and how she's giving one of them [another child] nightmares which make her wet the bed and making the other one cry and refuse to come to school. And they talked to me about it and I said, 'Well, I'll have a word with my head about it and see if there's anything we can do.' But then they took it upon themselves to say something to this little girl's mum that they didn't want her to play with them any more. It's very tricky.

Frequently there is not a lot you can do about such situations except put it down to experience, learn from it and move along.

Several books on control and discipline techniques are listed at the end of Chapter 2 but, before leaving the topic and, by way of introduction to the next section, Ulla voices a fairly common problem, 'I only find discipline stressful if I've got other people watching me'.

Help in the Classroom

Having a spare pair of adult hands in the classroom can often help reduce the stresses involved in sharing yourself between thirty or so children. It can also have some added benefits as Iona and Teresa describe.

If you have parents in, and they take a small group, they'll come in afterwards and say, 'I don't know how to manage with so and so. He wouldn't do what I asked him at all.' And I've had parents say to me, 'This has really opened my eyes'.

I felt when I came here initially that parents were very closely watching what I was doing and therefore I decided to welcome them in to the classroom with open arms. They did come in and share activities and, although it was a stress having them watch me, in the end it's paid off and I've got some lovely parents who are in there supporting and helping me which is very nice, but initially that was a big, big stress.

Janet says that she thinks it is very important that parents come and help in the classroom; after all, 'It's their children that we have got here'. Gavin agrees but adds that, while he's got a 'good batch of parents . . . it adds to the workload in that you have to organize what the helpers are doing.'

Sandra agrees that parents and welfare assistants can be an asset but it is a double-edged sword.

You've got to organize them as well as the class and the work doesn't quite get done as you would do. Sometimes it's easier just to do it yourself.

Another problem can arise when helpers try to talk to you while you are teaching.

I find Mrs H a very helpful person to have in the classroom but it is extremely distracting — not to say irritating — if she talks to me while I'm, for example, working with a group. The children aren't allowed to do it but I can hardly tell her, 'You know the rules. Get on with your work.' I have tried to ensure that she knows exactly what to do before we start the session but, almost invariably, a question will pop up just when I'm in full flow with a group.

In general the teachers seemed to appreciate extra help and some considered themselves to be extremely lucky:

I have an ancillary help on a Tuesday and Thursday afternoon and the rest of the time I have mother helpers who are brilliant.

Others were perhaps less fortunate:

I find parents are very happy to come on trips but I still haven't got anybody who is willing to come and help in the classroom.

A strategy here might be to try and recruit some grandparents or other senior citizens. Of course, as discussed in Chapter 2, it is as well that you do not advertise your desire for help too widely otherwise you might find yourself receiving an offer from a less than desirable volunteer!

A Veritable Juggling Act

Even when everything is running relatively smoothly teaching is a very demanding and potentially stressful profession as you '. . . just try to be on tap for so many children all the time'.

Olive says that sometimes she feels that things become fragmented,

. . . because you've got a lot of children buzzing around you and making incessant demands so you are not actually taking in what you want to take in necessarily.

Catherine finds it taxing,

> . . . keeping A and B from fighting over the bricks while you're trying to supervise C and D's writing or whatever it is they are doing.

And Penny thinks that sometimes,

> There is too much going on as one group are trying to do a science investigation and another table is trying to do some language. It is very hard, I find.

Sometimes the pressure builds up so much that Alex says,

> You have so much to do you get this 'fizzy brain syndrome' when, you know, everything seems to be vibrating.

Gavin seemed to be frustrated, saying,

> There is nothing in the job that can't be done given time. There's nothing too difficult to do. It's the time pressure that makes it difficult.

Ulla laughingly explained,

> In terms of organizing the children I'm not sure that that's always organized well because often I organize too many things that need me and then that becomes stressful. But I've always got everything that I need. I always know where everything is. I have all my pieces of paper in files that are marked so I can always get hold of them if I'm asked to do something. I'm very good. I'd be a wonderful bureaucrat. I'm fabulous with pieces of paper. It's the children I'm not very good with.

Brenda believes that,

> When you have too much to think about and you get to an overload situation that's where it pays to lessen the goal a bit.

She explained that sometimes,

> I'll do a whole class activity and then I know that each child has produced a piece of work. And then you look at the results —

I suppose that's the sad part — for you think, 'I could hav done better if I'd been teaching in a small group. They'd hav done a lot better than that'.

Tracy's strategy for dealing with classroom overload is less of a c scious one (literally!):

> If I'm stressed with a classroom often I find myself switching off. I suppose it's the mechanism to actually sort of stop you feeling more stressed. You tend to switch off and sometimes it's sort of like a dream situation when you're on automatic pilot and you're coping within the classroom. It's a level you actually work to so you have to let things pass you by and you have to let things sort of roll off you so you don't take yourself beyond that level where you're at screaming pitch.

After School

Many people think that once you have said goodbye to the last child and waved the last parent off the premises you can go home and put your feet up for the rest of the day. They seem to forget all the meetings, marking, paperwork, displays and so on and so on.
Norma bemoaned that sometimes,

> You hit a week where you've got everything in the world to mount and put on the wall.

Most teachers would like to change their displays more frequently and sometimes, as Iona, they feel that they have little option.

> . . . there was one picture, I think, which had a manger on. Well, obviously you can't keep that up for too long. In years past we've sometimes planned something for Christmas that could be left up for a bit longer.

Ulla is of the opinion that,

> People don't change displays in the way that they used to do and there's got to be a certain amount of mackling (i.e., throwing it together) to survive.

Brenda, however, feels uneasy about 'mackling' to survive for,

> You always feel judged and you always feel that you should be aware of how you are presenting to other people.

Added to which, as Paula and Iona describe, there can often be another problem.

> I had three meetings on the trot this week and I'm trying to put up the hall display and I'm thinking, 'When am I going to do it?'

> If you want to put something up on the wall in your classroom — something you've done that day — if there's a meeting after school you can't do it. Of course sometimes you do do it but it can be stressful if you can't take as much time and do it as carefully as you would like.

Reading the above remark, Daphne said,

> Well, why on earth doesn't she get the children to put up their own display? I certainly do. It may not be perfect but it gives them a sense of pride, saves me an incredible amount of time and, in any event, I can always spend a couple of minutes at the end of the day tidying it up a bit.

Staff meetings can also prove very time consuming. Some teachers seem to be lucky.

> The meetings we have I find are always useful and to the point . . . I never sit there and think, 'I could be doing this now,' or, 'Why am I here?'

But others are obviously less so.

> Meetings are stressful because there are so many of them and sometimes I wonder, 'What really did we decide at that meeting?' or, 'What a waste of time when I could have been doing something more more worthwhile.'

Out-of-school meetings were also perceived to be helpful by some.

> I always think I'm more stressed than other people until I go to meetings and courses and then someone says, 'Oh dear, I . . .' and then you find you are not alone.

Others seemed to find them more of a test of stamina.

> I've been to the Teachers' Centre and it's warm in there, and
> you have a nice cup of tea and a biscuit, and you sit down and
> somebody at the front starts to talk, and you're bombarded with
> paperwork, aren't you, all these handouts . . . and I sit there and
> I think, 'Oh no, I mustn't shut my eyes, because it looks so rude
> to the person at the front; they must think, "Gosh, am I really
> as boring as all this".' But it's just that time of the day, you really
> have had enough, and your brain, I don't think it takes as much
> in.

And then, of course, there is all the marking, assessment and paperwork, as Pat explains:

> I find there are lots of things you need to do: marking, going
> through things, writing up your notes, planning and so on and
> so on.

Gavin finds assessment particularly difficult because, unlike in second-
ary schools,

> . . . there is no slot in the school day when that can be done. So
> that's something that pushes itself into private time, evenings
> and weekends.

Some people are rather more casual in their approach.

> I'm one of these people who leaves it to the last minute for
> records. I do them half-termly rather than weekly although some
> weeks I might write something for a portfolio or some observa-
> tion or assessment.

Most of the teachers I spoke to agreed that there was too much
paperwork. Ulla considered,

> I could teach without having to put all that down on paper . . . all
> the assessment and all the record-keeping you've got to do
> takes a disproportionate amount of time . . . [although] I think it
> is important that you do have some evidence of the children's
> work.

And Steven announced,

> The biggest worry I find about paperwork is that when I talk to people no one ever reads what you've written down. You gather all this work together and pass it on but no one ever looks at it. Why do we bother? . . . But I guess that's something hopefully that will get resolved. You don't want a huge dossier on each child. You want a couple of clear sheets maybe with a few examples of work.

Joanne seemed less weighed down than some of her colleagues, believing that,

> Certainly the regular things that we have to do — like our planning files and our evaluation of what we've done — I think it's necessary, hard as it might be.

And Ulla is highly fortunate for, 'I quite like paperwork so I don't find it stressful'.

More about paperwork will be discussed when we focus on senior staff but let us not forget that many staff in primary schools also have posts of responsibility. Catherine, for example, is a teacher governor and is responsible for information technology and multicultural education in her school.

> The amount of paper that you get given to look at around here is horrific. I mean, just as an example, I get governors' papers, I get papers relating to IT, new software, hardware etc., and I get papers related to multicultural issues. As well as that there's assessment, national curriculum, and there just seem to be papers everywhere at home and at school. All the drawers are just filled with bits of paper. Now I know they're all — well some of them are useful and valuable — but it's this sort of information processing, there's just so much I don't have time to sit down and absorb the useful bits from it and sieve through it and chuck out the really irrelevant bits.

Some Final Comments

Teaching is, undoubtedly, highly demanding and, to end this chapter, here are some reflections.

It would be ideal if, in the classroom, it was just you and your kids getting on with the job to the best of your ability with no one interfering or telling you what you've got to do or how you've got to do it and what you'd got to record and all the other stuff. (Iona, after 30 years in the classroom)

I would say, 'Think very carefully before you become a teacher,' and, 'The most useful thing to me has been to be able to talk to people and discuss and go over things with them. Don't ever do it on your own. Don't be on your own basically.' (Marianne, with more than 20 years' experience)

I think many teachers are like me: they have this sort of professional perfectionism, if you like. You're always trying to do your best for every child in your class and there is just too much to do and never enough time to do it. (Teresa, after 'many' years in the classroom)

You must learn to set a limit and say 'no more'. (Olive, in her third year of teaching)

And finally, John Eggleston reminds us,

To be a teacher is like living a life dedicated to mission impossible . . . The satisfactions of teaching can be immense: no other profession can experience the immediate joy of children's new learning, understanding and fulfilment or see the long-term results of the commitments, enthusiasm or careers that are formed in the school. (1992, p.1)

Summary

- Everyone thinks he/she knows about teaching and has some advice for teachers!
- To an outsider you probably seem very calm and friendly and, perhaps contrary to your best interests, you almost certainly make the job look considerably easier than it is.
- You may not be able to do much about the size and location of your classroom but it might be possible to improve the atmosphere.

- Planning is a necessary evil, the burden of which can some-times be eased if you have congenial colleagues willing to pool ideas.
- Thinking children can be the joy and challenge of the job!
- Observation, intervention and matching are all essential but often hard.
- Difficult children tend to make huge demands on your time and energy but establishing good relationships with them can pay off.
- Start the year with clearly defined classroom rules and expecta-tions, convey them to your pupils and reward them accordingly.
- Having help in the classroom is usually a bonus but it can require considerable time and tact on your part.
- Classrooms are generally exceedingly busy places!
- The work certainly does not stop when the children go home and there can often be conflicting demands on your time.
- Young and old colleagues can sometimes offer some good advice!

Further Reading and References

Some of the following are mentioned in the text. All are accessible and all are written by people who seem to understand teachers are sympathetic towards them.

DESFORGES, C.W. (1995) *An Introduction to Teaching: Psychological Perspec-tives*, Oxford, Blackwell.

EGGLESTON, J. (1992) *The Challenge for Teachers*, London, Cassell.

EVERTSON, C.M. and HARRIS, A.H. (1992) 'What we know about managing classrooms', *Educational Leadership*, **49**, pp.74–8.

KYRIACOU, C. (1992) *Essential Teaching Skills*, Hemel Hempstead, Simon and Schuster Education.

LAAR, B., BLATCHFORD, R., WINKLEY, D., BADMAN, G. and HOWARD, R. (1989) *Effective Teaching*, Oxford, National Primary Centre.

MOYLES, J.R. (1992) *Organizing for Learning in the Primary Classroom*, Buckingham, Open University Press.

NEILL, S. and CASWELL, C. (1993) *Body Language for Competent Teachers*, London, Routledge.

PATERSON, K. (1993) *HELP! Survival Strategies for Teachers*, Markham, Ontario, Pembroke Publishers.

POLLARD, A. (1990) *Learning in Primary Schools*, London, Cassell.

Rowland, V. and Birkett, K. (1992) *Personal Effectiveness for Teachers*, Hemel Hempstead, Simon and Schuster Education.

Woods, P. (1990) *Teacher Skills and Strategies*, London, Falmer Press.

Wragg, E.C. (1993) *Classroom Management*, London, Routledge.

4   Staffrooms, Colleagues and Friends

In previous chapters I have touched on working with colleagues and getting to know new members of staff. Here I want to take a closer look at relationships and how they can enhance your working life or greatly add to your stress levels. For many it is a crucial issue. Indeed Brenda is convinced,

> . . . if schools can really create a climate where teachers can talk openly and freely I think stress levels would go.

Staffrooms

Staffrooms are curious places and there are huge variations between them. Some are vast, draughty barn-like rooms; others are little more than a cupboard; some are fitted out with comfortable chairs, microwaves, fridges (you name it, they have it) while others comprise a few very upright and hard-backed chairs. I suspect, to a certain extent, the appearance of the room does affect the atmosphere within it. But, having said that, only one of the teachers I spoke to actually mentioned any of the physical aspects of the staffroom. Moreover, it seems that where a staff are working well together, they will take the trouble to make the room look as attractive and comfortable as possible.

Apart from their more formal roles (a meeting room, a medical room, etc.) staffrooms appear to have three main functions when they are working well. They are a place in which you can relax:

> The only time I actually relax is when I go down and eat my lunch in the staffroom.

They are a place where you can let off steam:

> It's a very friendly staffroom where you can come and unburden a bit. If a certain young gentleman has filled my sink with glue yet again I can go and have a groan about it and everyone will be really nice and supportive.

And they are a place where you can talk:

> It's nice to be supportive and to be supported and if there's a problem to be able to talk about it.

Sometimes, however, they are places which are endeavouring to serve too many — often conflicting — functions at one time. Iona explains,

> And when the parents are in there obviously you can't sit there and have a moan or anything and at lunchtime quite often there's a kind of informal meeting about something. There's all sorts of discussions going on — talking shop really — and I don't know that that's a good thing. You want a complete break . . . [wistfully] We used to sit and have a chat about all sorts of things in the lunch hour and we don't do that now.

(Some of you might argue that lunch hours are a useful time to talk over work-related matters and perhaps they are but, as I will discuss in more detail later, I would also suggest that it is important that you take some time to switch off and relax during the day.)

Stephen remarked that, while perhaps the staffroom in his last school was a good place to let off steam, this was not compatible with other desirable functions.

> There were calm people there but there was a lot of hysteria as well. The staffroom was just so noisy. People were almost screaming because the children had got to them and tearing their hair out and even the laughter was so loud. I don't think it was my colleagues there. I don't think it was their normal personalities. I think the whole place was hyped up because it was such a hard school to teach in.

So what of the individuals who make up your staff?

Working Relationships

From observations and discussion it seems that, broadly speaking, you might find yourself with one of four types of colleague. The first category comprises people working together at their best and may be described by Olive, Catherine, Marianne and Katrina.

... everybody's very supportive, very friendly, nobody's condemning.

And you know that there will be someone within the group who will be able to answer a question you have. Whatever it is they are very supportive and will offer you alternative strategies.

People are very forthcoming here, very supportive. Brilliant. I've never known it before. I think you feel sometimes that if you're failing or that you need help, you just need someone to say, 'Am I doing all right?' You don't need to worry about it here because people do it automatically and they understand. And they are there to support you, which is what it's all about.

Here everyone listens to each other. They are really genuinely interested.

One of the distinctive qualities of such groups of people is that everything is very much a two-way process and all the participants willingly play equivalent — though not necessarily identical — roles.

To some, the second category of staff grouping may appear rather similar to the first. The difference is, however, that some of its members seem to be playing a greater supporting role than others:

Often all you are doing is just listening but the fact that they [other staff] are unloading on you is stressful.

Geoff falls into a similar category for, although he feels he can talk to colleagues, far more often than not he is on the receiving end of their woes:

Talking out problems with another member of staff is a mixed blessing. For when you want to talk it's helpful to talk but it's also a pressure on time when other people want to talk and you don't feel you've got time to talk to them. They'll pass my room. A lot of people come by and a lot of people stop off — as one did tonight — to talk about school and family problems and all sorts of things and I wanted to go home.

Fred, a headteacher, suffers a similar problem as other heads keep phoning him for advice and he explains it thus:

They will say to me, 'I can talk to you because you always seem so relaxed and so laid back'.

The difficulty is that,

> . . . after a while it gets to you because you start taking on board their problems and — although you keep telling yourself not to — you worry about them and then you ring them up and then you find you're involved in it.

I am not — I hasten to add — suggesting that you intentionally look stressed to discourage people from talking to you! Rather, as will be discussed in the last chapter, that you develop an appropriate balance.

The third type of grouping is probably the most stressful as, I suspect, it is rather like a running sore. Brenda is still in such a situation: 'Conflict with colleagues is a major source of stress unfortunately'. Marianne and Katrina no longer are but they can well remember what it was like.

> It's no good struggling on your own and that's bothered me in the past where I felt, 'I can't say that. I can't do this'. I felt very undervalued and by the beginning of the final year at my last school I was ready to give up teaching completely.

> It was very stressful at my old school because, at every opportunity, one particular member would have a swipe at me and she'd make a kind of joke of it. I began to think I'd got a real problem and that I really was all the things she kind of indicated I was. And it wasn't until I got away from that situation that I realized that it wasn't me at all.

And, finally, there are school staffs where there is little or no communication other than that which is considered essential. Some of these groups, I am sure, manage very well and see themselves as a happy community with few problems. Others, I suspect, are less content and may well be harbouring individuals who feel lonely and isolated. This brings us to the next section where I will examine some of the factors which seem to create difficulties in working relationships.

Dissecting the Distance between Colleagues

Wendy and Penny echo the thoughts of several of the teachers in less than happy schools.

> I very much feel that everyone is judging me all the time.

> I think you worry that you haven't done everything that you should do or you haven't had time to do everything that you should do. You feel perhaps if you haven't met a deadline, for instance, that people are going to think that you're inadequate.

Seemingly such individuals often can't or won't ask for help for a variety of very understandable reasons. One of these is, quite simply, that they perceive their colleagues as just too busy. When I asked Lorna whether there was anyone to whom she could talk to when feeling stressed she replied, 'Yes, I suppose I do talk to them but everyone's so busy there's not that much time'. Another reason for hesitations is that, especially when you are feeling low, other colleagues just seem so competent. This can result in your feeling that, although they might be kind to you, 'they wouldn't really understand'. But Yvonne, a successful head, explains,

> . . . even those who are managing the job will have had, at times, very low spots when they felt like jacking it in. And it's difficult to overcome the feeling that you're not succeeding and yet we have all felt it in some measure.

And Maria quite simply says,

> We all make mistakes. We can't all be brilliant all of the time.

Katrina cautions, however, that a one-way communications with colleagues may not be enough: sharing can be far more valuable.

> If I share things with people who seem to have it all sussed out it doesn't make me feel much better. One of the things that actually makes me feel better is knowing that other people have similar problems.

The fear of being judged as incompetent is another very real obstacle in asking for help. In many cases this may not be as justified as you think.

> I've discovered that you can talk to everybody. They're all sympathetic and helpful and nobody says, 'Oh dear, she can't cope,' or whatever.

I think you can feel you're alone and it's only you and you can't cope because you're not very able or something like that. You run yourself down and really it's everybody. Everybody's feeling the same.

The problem is that, even if you half believe what these teachers say, how can Anne Cockburn really believe that you will have the nerve to ask that old battleaxe for advice? How naïve can you get! To such accusations three courses of action spring to mind. The first is to talk to somebody else (possibly someone in another school or a sympathetic friend). The second is to consider whether you really want to stay in your particular job (see Chapter 8). And the third, and probably the most rewarding, is to stand back and try to view your relationship with colleagues as calmly and objectively as possible. Ask yourself, for example,

- Did the current headteacher appoint you to the school? (If so, he/she obviously rates you as a teacher.)
- Are your colleagues kind to their pupils? (I suspect that, as primary teachers, the vast majority are.) What makes you think that they will be unkind to you?
- What aspects of their behaviour are putting you off talking to them? (Perhaps it is the way that they snap or make sarcastic remarks. Could these be symptoms of their own tension or insecurities?)
- Have you had a 'dust-up' in the past and do you think old grievances might linger on? Or perhaps there is even an on-going feud? (Aronson's book listed at the end of the chapter can provide often amusing insights into what people tend to do when they have made a decision or stated a point of view: they usually become more and more convinced that they are right despite lack of further evidence!)
- Are you worried that they might pass on your concern? (If they gossip about other people this may well be a justified anxiety and I would be inclined to select someone else to confide in.)
- Are you concerned that they might not be sympathetic? (Perhaps you could try them with a small problem first and see how they react.)
- Do you think that they might have difficulty in coping? (You might be surprised! For example, Alice describes herself as a 'happy worrier'. All her own worries are well aired in the staffroom and, as a result, she feels much better and is more than able to cope with other people's concerns.)

- Is there a part of you that really feels that it is not up to you to ask for help but for others to offer it? (Perhaps you give the impression of being rather dauntingly in control and have what Rona describes as 'an impregnable exterior'.)

At the end of the day it might be that you just cannot confide in your colleagues. But, as will be discussed below and in the final chapter, it is almost certainly a good idea to talk to someone. It may be that they can provide some valuable feedback or it might be a mechanism for letting of steam or sorting out your thoughts. Simon is clear, 'I think you need to talk to somebody about it at the end of the day. Even if it's just the cat or the goldfish.'

The Value of Good Relationships

Obviously if a staff works well together as a team everyone tends to feel happier and more content than they might do otherwise. It seems that good staff relationships can also serve four other important functions.

The first is really pragmatic: John Eggleston explains,

> Schools are now, more than ever, being run as businesses. Each teacher is an important manager in a team that is generating a product, helping to market it and jointly responsible for the success and failure of the enterprise. (1992, p.71)

In part, the National Curriculum and all the recent changes in our educational system have encouraged this coming together but I think it has always been true that some schools, such as Gordon's, have planned at least some things together:

> As a staff we agree that the hall will have new displays and we have a day when it will be done.

A second, and very important, function of a good staff is that they are willing to help one another out in times of difficulty. Again, Gordon explains,

> Support from others is important. Today I had some practical help as I had a head cold and the teacher next door said, 'Oh

well, mine are watching a video at the end of the afternoon and your class can come in for half-an-hour then'. There's quite a lot that goes on. If someone is feeling that they need to have a break or they need more time to do something we can double up the class and take them all in the hall and do something.

Perhaps some parents might not approve of such doubling-up of classes but I would suggest that it is infinitely better than a teacher having a breakdown or simply having to take several weeks off when a neglected cold becomes pneumonia. Thus an effective staff can help minimize the negative effects of each other's mood swings and ill health.

Leading on from this, a third function is to help one another find solutions to a problem and not merely tackle the symptoms. Alice and Brenda both encourage an honest approach.

I would hate to have to keep up a front. I think it's really important to be able to discuss where you think you're falling down.

I find the best way to deal with the stresses involved is to talk to other teachers and to try to be as open as possible.

Talking in this way often includes overlap with the fourth function which is to provide reassurance and support to each other. As Brenda says,

The talking helps but also knowing that people have been there before.

Jane echoes her thoughts,

I like to hear what other people have been doing in our staffroom: perhaps offloading about somebody and, if it's somebody I've had before, I can say, 'Well, yes, he did this when I had him'. Then they can reply, 'Oh, he's still doing it', and that sort of thing is quite reassuring.

It may be that, although caring, your staff lack some of the skills to perform all four of these functions but, with the help of good leadership (see next chapter), thought and perhaps some inset, I think you will find that the benefits far outweigh the effort of acquiring the necessary expertise.

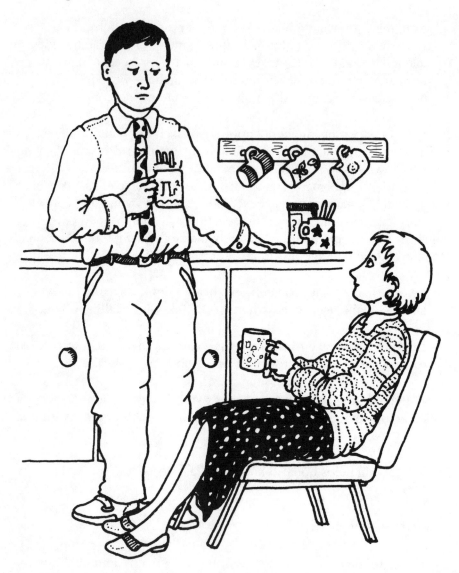

Figure 4.1: It's comforting to talk to other people

In Times of Difficulty

In this final section I thought it would be useful to consider how usually effective schools and individuals behave when there appears to be trouble on the horizon. If there is a storm brewing up these three practitioners are quite clear,

> If we disagree on something, we usually speak out and that tends to avoid things building up.

> Sometimes you can't avoid conflict and it's not right to do so.

> I don't like conflict. [How do you deal with it then?] Talk, talk, talk, talk, talk. Try and talk it out. Try and resolve it all the time.

Similarly, if you as an individual have a problem, the advice is seemingly clear and consistent, as three other individuals explain.

> Sometimes talking to other heads can actually raise your stress because you can be made aware of things that you are not doing that you should be doing. But equally it can be helping you to get a sense of proportion that somebody else is not actually doing the things that you're not doing as well.

> I talk to other members of staff. I talk to my husband and any of my friends who might enquire — anybody really who I speak to who shows an interest in what I'm doing.

> It's comforting to talk to other people because you realize that it's not just you. You tend to think when you're all in a frazzle, 'Crumbs, I must be getting too old, or I'm not right in the job, or I'm a square peg in a round hole.' But then when you hear other people you think, 'Oh well, it isn't just me. It's general'.

This approach, however, does not necessarily suit everyone all of the time. Simon, for example, would rather have peace and quiet and, accordingly, he has his lunch as soon as the bell goes rather than wait for other members of staff to gather.

> I can go and eat my lunch on my own and no one bothers . . . just no noise and to get away from everyone is pretty good.

Nor should you feel that talking things through automatically means that you need take their advice: it might, however, help calm you down and clarify your thoughts, as this interview with Hilda illustrates.

> *Anne:* How do you deal with stress?
> *Hilda:* I talk.
> *Anne:* To whom? To yourself?
> *Hilda:* Not yet! I talk to my husband . . . I can't always accept advice about a problem but I just need to talk about it. And if I'm stressed I don't always deal with it immediately. I have to go away and think something through. Part of the stress is knowing that if you snap or respond in a high-handed way it can be counterproductive so you've got to think of a way round it that's going to get you to the end you actually want to meet.

And finally, as discussed earlier in the chapter, you may need to select your listener(s) with care if you are in a less than sympathetic environment. As we see below, Ulla confides in ex-college friends but, to ensure absolute confidentiality, you could approach a counsellor, priest or a number of other professionals.

> I'm lucky having friends like Sally and Sue who understand what I'm talking about and it won't go any further. You need that because it's so incestuous in teaching. I mean, you can so easily say the wrong thing to the wrong person and the tom-toms are at it.

Follow-up Questions

- Does your staffroom endeavour to serve too many (usually conflicting) functions at one time?
- Do you play the role of talker and listener in approximately equal measures?
- Do you and your colleagues communicate effectively in a supportive manner?
- Which, if any, of these roles do you and your colleagues play: judge, jury or accused?
- Do you make time for one another?
- Are your colleagues generally sympathetic human beings?

- Do you share successes and failures?
- Do you work as a team?
- Do you talk enough?
- There are people to whom you can talk: how many of them have you met?
- Do most of your responses leave you feeling depressed? If so, what do you propose to do about it?

Further Reading and References

Jennifer Nias (1989) has written a book which explains many of the issues discussed in this chapter. It is entitled *Primary Teachers Talking*, published by Routledge.

The two references mentioned in the text are:

ARONSON, E. (1972) *The Social Animal*, San Francisco, Freeman and Company. (It may be old and out of print but it is good and worth searching out in the library)
EGGLESTON, J. (1992) *The Challenge for Teachers*, London, Cassell.

5 The Trials and Tribulations of Senior Staff

I have never been a headteacher so perhaps this, of all the chapters, is the most presumptuous. I have, however, observed and spoken to numerous heads, deputies and their colleagues in my time.

The title of the chapter is intentionally ambiguous. There is no doubt that senior staff can create trials and tribulations for their junior colleagues and vice versa. This chapter has certainly not been written exclusively for headteachers and their deputies. Obviously it is intended to be of value to them but, perhaps more importantly, it has been designed to broaden our understanding of staff relationships and stresses and strains within the hierarchical system of primary, first or middle schools.

For many, the headteacher of a school plays a crucially important role.

> I think the headteacher really is the pivot.

> I have been in schools where headteachers have given me an awful lot of stress and then it's really difficult to claw your way in every day. I mean, to me it's not worth it. To me, if there's a problem with my head I would rather just leave.

And yet Cary Cooper and Mike Kelly write,

> The training and development provision for senior managers in education has traditionally been haphazard and thinly spread. (1993, pp.130–43)

So what is it like starting out as a new head or deputy with little or no training?

Early Days

I touched on starting out as a senior member of staff in Chapter 2. Whether you are new to the school or have been promoted from within the ranks, the first few months are often filled with some exciting new challenges and some highly stressful and lonely moments. If you have been promoted from within you have the distinct advantage of knowing your colleagues; you may also, however, have to cope with having to adjust your relationship with staff now that you are in a 'position of authority'. Jealousy might also be an issue if another colleague was competing for the same job. And there may be one or two people who feel that, 'It is a pity we didn't get some fresh blood into the place.'

Coming in from outside presents its own problems. Teresa describes her first term as a deputy head,

> There was a new school to take on board, a new building, new routines. There were new children that I hadn't met before, a new class to become accustomed to, new relationships with parents to build, and that's always difficult, I think, when you're establishing a rapport with them. It's a very sort of stressful thing. And then there was actually, apart from that side of it, the new role of the deputy and building relationships with staff, and a relationship with the head, and you've got that sort of middle role always, haven't you, which is always very difficult to balance, I think, and that was very stressful.

Added to which she found herself thinking,

> 'I wonder what they're thinking about me. Am I doing the right thing? Am I doing a good job? What's going on in their minds?' And again with the head, 'What does she think of me? How am I doing? Am I doing all right?' That was a constant stress.

Perhaps had other staff been more supportive and complimentary (see below) she might have found it easier to be more open and honest. Fortunately, after a term, she says,

> I'm feeling more relaxed now with the people here and in going to the staffroom and being able to say those sort of things, 'Oh, gosh, I've had an awful morning'. I couldn't have done that in the beginning because I felt that they would have looked at me and thought, 'Who's she coming in, the new deputy, and she can't control a class, and she's had a bad day,' so I couldn't actually unwind and relax.

Edna, a headteacher, echoes Teresa's feelings,

> I remember when I first became a head my first assembly hung
> over me because I felt everybody would be watching . . . I felt,
> as a new headteacher, very much on my own.

Katrina and Harriet, both headteachers, found that it took far longer
than they expected to settle in to any routine simply because there was
so much to learn.

> I think probably the first six months to a year of headship are
> very stressful and then maybe, as you experience more situa-
> tions, it gets easier. I suppose it's the newness of the experience
> that's stressful . . . A lot of the experiences you haven't had before
> so you haven't got any experience to draw on.

> When you first start the job there are lots of new things to cope
> with and there are lots of surprises because you don't anticipate
> things happening. For the first 18 months I seemed to have to
> scramble through things and scraped by by the skin of my
> teeth. It was crisis management all the way.

I suspect few, if any, teachers appreciate how very difficult it is for
new senior staff to settle in, especially as — and this will be discussed
below — the majority of people feel that it is important to appear
confident and in control.

By the same token, new heads in particular need to be sensitive to
the anxiety they may create in their staff. It is almost inevitable that you
will want to make changes and most people will be expecting as much;
but, as discussed in Chapter 7, change is seldom easy and can take
considerable time and energy. Sam explained the frustration of his new
headteacher coming in with a new broom in Chapter 2 (p.32). Here
Gavin discusses the stress created by his new head,

> One of things that's being re-negotiated at the moment that I
> find stressful is assemblies. Because one of the things that we
> agreed before the new head came was a basic format for assem-
> blies, and we talked a lot about prayers and the difference
> between collective worship and corporate worship. There was
> a lot of difference about what should be going on, but we
> reached an understanding whereby everybody was content with
> what was going on. So it was a work arrangement. And our
> new head, of course, wasn't party to all that and has come in
> with her ideas and it's one of the things that hasn't yet been

re-negotiated. She's being very sensitive to all the feelings in the school. I have an anxiety that we've got to go through that delicate business of negotiating again and we might come up with a different outcome that I would be less happy with.

In time, with luck, everyone settles down. But, as we see, Iona hopes her headteacher will learn to relax:

Probably because June is a new head she needs to cross every t and dot every i, even down to having our staff meetings minuted. Everything has got to be in place.

On Being a Deputy Headteacher

A deputy headship is often seen simply as a stepping-stone. However, one of the headteachers I spoke to spontaneously remarked,

I think being a deputy is probably the most difficult job in the world. As a deputy you are always having to fit in with people.

She went on to explain,

. . . because when you're a deputy you're trying to do two jobs. You're trying to help, be part of the management team, do all the liaison and the listening and the sharing and the communicating that's involved in that job. And yet you're trying also to be a good classroom practitioner. And part of being a good classroom practitioner is actually getting displays up and making them look wonderful, and getting them up when the children have done the work, and making it all meaningful and making it look beautiful, and displays are one of the things that I feel say an enormous amount about a class teacher. I always used to feel terribly guilty and terribly aware if somebody came in and a display had been up for a long time. I was always apologizing.

Teresa feels much the same,

I'm ashamed of the display in my classroom. I've got a big guilt thing about that, but it's hard when I'm concentrating on the children and organizing their days and being a deputy and taking assembly or talking to the head or what have you.

Ulla explains that she finds it very stressful being a deputy as,

> I don't have enough time to do the job that I feel I ought to be
> doing as a classroom teacher, and so I feel I do a really poor
> job at that because I've got to have some slack to go into, to
> doing the deputy heading bit.

Both Teresa and Ulla feel that it is important that they provide good
examples of classroom practice. They also see their roles as sounding
boards for both their headteachers and the staff but, as Ulla explains,
this can be very time consuming.

> I don't feel that I spend enough time listening to the head and
> supporting her, and all the time she's talking my head's thinking
> about something else and I'm not really concentrating on what's
> bothering her. I also find that I've got my agenda, but my agenda
> always seems to get waved out of the way, not intentionally, by
> other people. The head needs to talk to me now about this, and
> so the things that you were going to do have to go by the by.
> And we don't have enough time to talk things through, so it's
> permanently sort of grabbing a moment, and I never really
> understand what's going on because I only get bits of it. I don't
> get it into a total perspective. And the same with other members
> of staff: you know, you can think to yourself, 'I'll just go into the
> staffroom and cut that bit of paper, then I can go back and do
> so-and-so,' and somebody needs to talk to you. Or even if they
> don't say, 'Can I talk to you?' it develops into something that
> they obviously need to unload, and that I find really hard, that
> I've got my agenda up here but somehow I never seem to get
> round to it because of everyone else.

(As will be seen, headteachers generally very much appreciate their
deputies taking on this role of listener.)
  Other important functions of a deputy are to act as a curriculum
leader and encourage staff development. These involve considerable
reading ('It's no good my just being able to speak from a reception
point of view') and they also, understandably, seem to involve one
putting on an act, as Wendy explains,

> I think that's one of the reasons why I don't feel that I can sit
> in the staffroom and say, 'Oh God, this is going all wrong and
> I can't cope,' because I feel that if I start to look as though I'm
> falling apart, then what hope is there for them?

Unfortunately, such apparent confidence can backfire,

> I'm not very confident. People never believe it, and if I have to do birthday assembly when the head is out and it's the school, the teachers and parents, it's fine, but I worry about it before-hand. People always say, 'It's really easy for you,' and I think, 'Well, it's not'. I often give people the wrong impression that I'm very confident and I can do anything.

On a more positive note, most of the heads I have spoken to very much appreciate their deputies. To take two examples,

> Having someone you can talk things through with confiden-tially and whom you can really trust is incredibly important.

> I have to say that one of the things that's helped with reducing stress is having a deputy head who I really get on with and who I share decisions with. That has helped tremendously. And just before Christmas when I had to go away, I talked to her about what needed to be done and I walked out and I didn't worry about it. I knew there was somebody there who was doing things, not exactly the way I would do them, but we have got a shared understanding of how things should be and I knew if there was a distressed parent she would deal with them in the way I would deal with them, so that's been tremendous. That's made a lot of difference.

Having a good deputy after a mediocre one, '. . . is like having a pain and you don't realize until it's gone away'.

Some Headteachers' Priorities

Edna, the headteacher who made the last comment, was not involved in the selection of her previous deputy. She, as Katrina explains, sup-ports the following approach,

> When you're interviewing for new members of staff, I'm look-ing as much for personality as I am for expertise . . . The most important thing in a school is the relationships: the relationships between the children, the relationships between the teachers and all the parents. If that is working well you can actually cope

with the stresses because you're feeling supported and you feel you are supporting each other within that community.

Edna feels much the same and says,

What I really like is this sense of belonging and building up a team of people and working very closely with a team of people who all have similar aims.

Andrea expresses her prime aspiration slightly differently,

I want people to think, 'What a lovely school it is': not how good I am, but what a lovely school. And I want the children to remember. Because it's not just what you teach them; it's the way they think and what school is to them. It's such a responsibility.

Few of the headteachers I spoke to were so specific as to their aims but many of their thoughts are implicit in the next section, which focuses on headteacher stress. Having insight into someone's aims, aspirations, stresses and strains can be an important step to working effectively with them.

The Stresses and Strains of Being a Headteacher

The headteachers in the study volunteered eleven main sources of stress. Some of them are interrelated and all of them affected several, if not all, of the headteachers I interviewed.

Given the barrage of paper emanating from the Department for Education and elsewhere, it is perhaps not surprising that many heads find the volumes of *paperwork* a source of stress.

I find the mountains of paper really stressful, trying to keep on top of it all. There's a load of documentation that I know I ought to have within school but I don't have.

Some, such as Edith, find it helpful to remember,

It's a legal requirement and I've got to do it. In a jokey sort of way people say, 'Well, of course, if we didn't do it how would anybody know?' But even that's changing because of school inspections.

Aileen is more cynical,

> There's nothing more frustrating than knowing that you've sat
> for two hours writing something that will probably go into the
> filing cabinet and not be seen again.

Paperwork may be stressful, but it is quickly put aside when *relationships with staff* require attention. These, too, are often a source of anxiety.

> It is the day-to-day thing of working closely with people. There
> was an incident yesterday where one member of staff was very
> upset because of what somebody else had said to somebody
> else — and that's stressful because, well, how do you deal with
> it? Do you ignore it or do you then get involved in this, 'She
> said, I said, he said'? So I suppose the other stressful bit is
> knowing how to respond appropriately to other people's prob-
> lems. And how to respond to the person who you know has
> really got a problem; but they're not really acknowledging a
> problem, that's the biggest, that's the most difficult one of all.

Fred likes,

> . . . to think that this school is fairly successful. If I'm right in my
> thinking it's because the teamwork is right. The relationships
> are right. Keeping those relationships going is the hardest task.

Harriet very much feels that relationships between teachers and their headteachers should be mutually supportive. If they are not — for whatever reason — her stress levels increase,

> If I feel I don't have support I do get stressed by that, but I try
> not to do anything unless I'm sure people do support me . . .
> What really does stress me out is when I find I haven't got
> the staff's support when I thought I had.

This will be discussed in further detail below.

Parents have already been discussed in Chapters 2 and 3. Most heads seem to find them a problem from time to time, but Fred feels in a particularly difficult position as,

> The school is in an area of upper middle-class and aspiring
> middle-class parents. Very, very demanding. But it's also an

area where they house problem families. So our catchment area is very diverse. We've got children who would fit quite happily in the poorest city areas and we've got children who are likely to leave us for private schooling, or come to us from private schooling, where parents are very, very demanding: that's the only word for it. And questioning. Parents who will support the Gillian Shepherd moves, the Patten moves, the Kenneth Clarke-type moves to the hilt, and will come and talk to me and will pull out of a top pocket the Mail on Sunday opinion column which is their opinion too. And that can all be stressful, trying to listen to them and give them a say without giving them a total say.

Governors, with their wide range of skills, knowledge and experi-ence, can sometimes place high demands on headteachers too,

You've got to handle governors' questions tactfully but as hon-estly as you can. It's very difficult to keep people on a profes-sional line when they're not professionals themselves or working at that level.

Fortunately this is not always a problem,

Governors can be stressful. On the whole I've got a very good team of governors now who I think are very supportive. The last lot didn't give that feeling.

And, perhaps even more surprisingly, another headteacher was per-fectly serious when she said, 'Some things some find stressful others don't. I love governors' meetings. I adore them!'

Colleagues, parents and governors were specifically mentioned as three human sources of stress but, I suspect, Kate's more general state-ment is probably even more representative of the reality,

If I was failing in a relationship it would worry me enormously. I'd find it very, very stressful whether it was with a parent, with a child, with a staff colleague or anyone in fact. That probably bugs me more than anything.

As will be discussed later in the chapter, the headteachers I worked with were very anxious to foster their colleagues' confidence and boost their morale. They became very heated when the issue of the *media* was raised. Hugh and Fred explain why they are so angry,

My stress levels go up with media coverage. I think a lot of the things spoken by politicians don't marry up with reality in the job and the blanket statements made about the profession just don't ring true with my own experience.

The staff by and large know they do a good job, if you force them to say it, but they are a terribly insecure bunch, a lot of them. They feel of no value. And I find it very stressful when I'm constantly trying to praise them, thank them, build them up, and then you get some clown on the television saying that, 'We're going to get back to basics,' and, 'We're going to do this, that and t'other'.

Unfortunately, these politicians and 'clowns' have a lot of power. No one went into details about their views on government spending but it is clear that many were very concerned about their *budgets*.

I don't want to go for competitive tendering, I don't want to be involved in finding a 'good deal', but also when you're faced with about 20 pages of heretofores and whatever, it's jargon and you feel there's no will and there's no urgency, there's no immediate need to actually get to grips with it. I just put it away. That's an example of exactly what has fazed me recently. I have had it out three times and tried to listen to people explaining it to me and I just can't . . .

We've got the budget coming up soon. That is going to cause a lot of stress because there is not the money . . . We may be in the position of losing a whole member of staff which would be an enormous amount of stress.

Many leave their budget until the last minute, some because they seem to work best when the pressure is on and others because they have been 'attacked' by what Donald calls 'time bandits'. More specifically, he goes on,

Time bandits who are there actually, through no fault of their own, who are saying, 'We want to encroach on that pre-agreed and pre-planned timetable. We want your time now,' and they have every right to demand that time now because we can come in with an agreed strategy on the day where things are given priority, and that priority goes out of the window when the first parent comes in with an urgent need to talk about their particular problem.

Time will be discussed more fully in the next chapter. The lack of it, together with a seemingly endless list of deadlines, seems to create considerable stress for some headteachers.

I suppose it's deadlines I find stressful. If you know, for example, you've got a governors' meeting and you haven't done the headteachers' report. You feel an enormous sense of relief when you do get it done.

The real problem seems to be that there is just so much to do and no time in which to do it or, for that matter, in which to relax and recover.

When I was a class teacher there were some days when you could feel, 'I'm really pleased with that. It's finished. I can go home and forget about it.' Those days disappeared as a deputy. And I can't remember now what they felt like because as a head that's dreamland.

In some respects this *overload* is due to the relative lack of secretarial and administrative help found in the vast majority of our primary schools. The problem is even worse if you are a teaching head,

Because it's a small school the contact times are dinner times and break times so I get all the phone calls then. If someone's phoned me I have to phone them back at lunchtime. You have your preparation for the afternoon to do. That's when visitors tend to come. The dinner ladies come in and say, 'So-and-so's done so-and-so'.

Overload also seems to result from the fact that,

As a headteacher everything comes to me. There is so much to read and then I have to decide what I have to attend to, what needs to be passed on to the staff and what can be binned.

Overload, I suspect, is often closely linked with the *unpredictability* of the job which, as Victoria illustrates, can also prove stressful.

I suppose what I find stressful is the variety of things you have to tackle within a day. One minute you can have your hand thrust down a drain that's blocked on the playground and the next minute you are coping with quite complex curriculum issues or you're coping with personnel difficulties. So it's that variety and the way in which you have to leap from one thing to another at a moment's notice.

Many of these activities involve *decision making* and this is yet another source of stress.

I find making decisions is terribly hard. I don't mean the every-day bread-and-butter decisions. I mean the real decisions like, 'Do we need to lose a member of staff?'

Hilary finds it even more of a problem for she feels,

You get to saturation point with decision making, don't you, when you have to choose between chips and mashed potato. 'Somebody choose for me because I can't do it any more.'

And of course, with decision making comes *responsibility* and this too is sometimes perceived as highly stressful for, as a head, 'You always have that ultimate responsibility'. And, whether it is always appropriate or not, this lays you open to blame, as Fred remarks when discussing his budget decisions,

At the end of the day it will be regarded as my decision, as everything is . . . It's the same with class organization. The parents who don't approve of it pin it all on me, and the staff who say, 'Oh, I've got a mixed age group', pin it all on me, and everyone sort of stands back and holds me responsible.

Not only do headteachers have considerable responsibility but it seems that teachers — and even heads themselves — make various *assumptions* about the person who fills the role of 'headteacher'. For example, it appears that many feel that the head should always be available for them; that the head always behaves as a responsible professional; that the head can always manage everything, and so on and so forth. As Victoria describes, assemblies can be a daunting experience, especially if staff are in attendance.

I think assemblies can be very stressful. I certainly didn't like them when I first started and I'm much better at them now. But if you're left alone in a room with 200 children it can be quite demanding to actually hold 200 children for 20 minutes. If you're there with your staff it can be quite stressful: it is a kind of performance, just as classroom teaching can be a kind of performance. You're on show really, and if you're seen to be failing then it's a very public way in which to be failing.

Kate agrees, but adds that sometimes her fears get out of proportion.

I've talked to lots of heads about the things they found most stressful on becoming a head, and they all felt the same: assemblies. Because you have recurring nightmares of the whole school going out of control. And it's all in the mind. And then when it actually happens, when you actually come into school and do the assemblies, I thoroughly enjoy them. It's all in the mind beforehand. Once I'm into the term I don't mind them at all. It's only after a holiday like that when I think, 'Can I still do it?'

As if those stresses and strains were not enough, it seems almost universal that headteachers feel 'isolated and unappreciated' from time to time! Fortunately most of them are also resilient people who have some realistic suggestions which will be discussed in the next section.

Tried and Tested

Earlier in the chapter I mentioned the unpredictability of the job but, nevertheless, the more relaxed heads seemed to find that there were distinct advantages in being *well planned*.

I would say that I was very well organized and that's one of the tools I use to control my stress.

Donald describes how long-term planning is helpful.

I think the way we plan things at school now, and particularly in the way we go about our management planning, we forecast, as well as anybody ever could in any school, events as we are going to tackle them over a 24-month period. You say this is a priority for this year, and these are four or five issues that we are very much going to look at this year; if anything new then arrives — and we are beginning to be able to predict when documents are coming through and when documents are going to be changed — if that happens then you say, well, we can slot that in. And I think with that style of planning it makes the, shall we say, hot spots, easier to see when they're coming. Now, I know there will be a hot spot around about Easter, and there-fore I can avoid putting any extra pressures on then, unless it is an emergency, of course!

An added advantage to long-term planning is that, by spreading the load, staff are less likely to become ill: seemingly, if one operates a stress–slack–stress sequence, some individuals invariably get sick in the slack periods!

Victoria has a highly organized diary system which will be discussed in detail in the next chapter, but her basic principle is,

I try to plan where the pressures may be in a week and build in some slack so that if there is a crisis you always know you've got a little section of time where you can achieve those things you really have to achieve by the end of the week.

Intelligent planning — as discussed in previous chapters — can be a real boon for heads, teachers and even deputies, as Teresa concluded, 'I think careful planning has reduced a lot of stress'. Ideally planning should include a whole school policy on control and discipline for, as discussed in Chapter 3, the most effective practitioners have a manage-ment strategy in place before their pupils arrive each year. Moreover, Evertson and Harris (1992) stress that a whole school policy that every-one has planned is more likely to work and have credibility with the children.

Appropriate delegation also seemed to be an extremely worthwhile activity. Indeed Harriet believes,

I think the role of the head has changed so dramatically into more of a management role that you can't do the impossible. You've got to delegate.

Victoria finds it impossible to wade through all the National Curriculum documents and argues,

I think heads also have to accept that they cannot keep up with that, that they actually have to delegate that, and be quite clear in their discussions with teachers that the postholder for science or maths, or history, or whatever, is actually responsible for knowing that document and guiding other staff through it.

One of the great benefits of delegating, Harriet discovered, was, 'The deputy stopped criticizing me after she'd done the job for a few weeks when I was ill!'

Maintaining *good communication* was also seen as highly important by the headteachers. This means talking things through with your deputy — 'She is an ear for me and tells me if she feels the load is too much or somebody needs extra help' — but also ensuring 'an open dialogue with staff and open channels for people to say what they feel'.

Throughout the day all manner of things happen and ideas pop up, so people like Kate find it very helpful to have an *aide memoire*.

There are times when I've got about ten things going through my mind simultaneously and the way round that is to make notes each time. So if something comes to you and you write it down, it stops it running around in here [points to head] and you can stop thinking about it for a while, as you know you won't lose it.

As discussed in Chapter 1, you may not have a piece of paper to hand when you have your inspiring thoughts but there are usually ways round that, such as leaving reminders in conspicuous places or using mnemonics.

As all these thoughts, etc., come piling in, it is important to *prioritize effectively*. Wendy explains how she tackles the paperwork in this way,

Another management technique for coping with too much is to actually go through the pile of papers — and you see a big pile sitting on there — and quite carefully order which you will read, and when. When have you got to make a response to the White Paper? If it's next week then it's the first thing you read; the others drop to the bottom of the pile.

Katrina — echoing the views of all the heads I spoke to — was quite clear as to what came top of her list of priorities,

The children come first. Your colleagues come first. The paper can wait.

This can mean that, at times, she is totally swamped by paperwork, and her response to that is, 'Subvert the system!'

Indeed it seems a common, and necessary, survival strategy to *postpone* some of the less essential paperwork. Harriet says, 'We got on the last stage of appraisal by ignoring the letter'. And Fred explains,

> Now, I long ago decided that the people who work here come first, and if I get time I'll complete a form, and if I don't get time then it doesn't get completed. If it's really urgent they'll send me another one. And then if it's desperate they'll probably phone as well.

Interestingly, he goes on,

> One summer, when I was sorting things out, I found all sorts of forms and I thought, 'Oh God, I should have sent that back,' and, 'Oh heck, that should have gone'. And then I suddenly realized no one had ever chased me, no one had ever asked me, so how important was it in the first place?

And indeed, none of the heads I spoke to reported (admitted?) that they had been rapped on the knuckles or penalized for either the delay or the non-return of certain forms.

Obviously, sometimes the paperwork cannot be completely ignored and then it is important to *find a suitable place to work*. When discussing the matter with an adviser, Fred recalls being asked,

> 'Where are you trying to do it [the paperwork]?' and I said, 'Well, at school,' and he said, 'What happens when you're trying to do that at school?' I said, 'What do you mean, what happens?' He said, 'Well, how many times does somebody knock on the door? How many times does the phone ring? How many times does somebody say, 'So-and-so's had an accident, can you come?' Is it still dealt with?' and I said, 'Yes.' 'Right,' he said, 'do the work at home.' I said, 'Well, I don't know if I can do that.' 'Why not?' And after a while I began to think, 'Well, why not?' And so when I had to get this particular piece of work done I took the computer home and I stayed at home for two days. I got the work done and the school carried on.

It is often a good idea — perhaps particularly when you are feeling stressed — to *stand back* and consider the situation calmly and objectively from a distance. Harriet believes, 'Heads need the ability to stand back and analyse situations'. And Victoria sometimes takes this one step further,

> It's always interesting to hear about how people in other walks of life handle, say, personnel difficulties and that sort of thing. It helps to give you a wider perspective.

Standing back can also have the added advantage that it can create,

> Laughter! And being able to laugh at yourself and the whole situation is very therapeutic.

More pompously put, *keep things in perspective*. Enid and Kirsty are adamant that,

> It is very important to be somebody other than a headteacher.

And,

> You've actually got to say, in order to do this job well I've actually got to have some time to myself.

Fred finds a useful technique to restore the balance is,

> . . . to try and get away from anything that might be stressing you and have a walk by the sea or what have you.

And, if this is not possible, *visit a classroom*, for Fred defies anyone,

> . . . to still be stressed if you can go and talk to a 5 or 6 year old. I don't think it's possible!

Headteachers and Teachers

Now that we have considered some of the ways in which headteachers can help themselves, let us examine what they endeavour to do to support and assist their staff. It has been said that,

> . . . organisations and people within them are still often reluctant to take the problem of undue stress seriously. (Fontana, 1989, p.17)

Talking to headteachers over the years, however, I would have to say that the vast majority seem to put considerable effort into easing their colleagues' load. One effective way of doing this, Kate suggests, is to try,

> . . . to ensure that things that stressed you as a teacher are reduced for your staff.

Brenda, a teacher in her third year, considers,

> A lot of things heads do can be stress-relievers because they are practical.

Some of these practical gestures may go unnoticed but are none-theless important. These include ensuring that equipment is regularly serviced and in a good state of repair, minimizing the amount of record keeping, fairly and appropriately distributing administrative documents to be read, providing a list of notable events in the week, organizing that the school is a clean and safe environment in which to work. (Some might argue that it is trivial but it is amazing how a posy of flowers and some decent biscuits in the staffroom can cheer people up.) Devising an appropriate strategy for wet playtimes can also help staff considerably. Victoria, for example, says,

> If it's raining at breaktime I will elect to do an assembly on my own while the staff have a bit of a break and grab a cup of coffee.

At Simon's school, at wet playtimes, 'Welfare staff take over so we get a proper break'.

Several headteachers acknowledge the heavy burden of paper-work which teachers now have to complete. Brenda reports that she knows of some

> . . . schools where the head takes the whole school for half an hour before lunch on a Monday to allow the teachers to plan.

Headteacher Fred takes it a step further,

> I'm saying more and more to my staff, 'If you've got a policy document to write you mustn't write it at home in the evenings. Ask for the day off.' Then either I go in and cover for them or

we find a supply from somewhere. It makes the staff feel that the writing of a policy document is a professional thing and therefore they're being given time to do it. It makes them feel they've been given a bonus and so they feel a bit happier. I think it also enables them to have a breather from the classroom.

(Some might question whether Fred has not gone a little too far but it provides him with valuable classroom experience and — if you want to be pragmatic — a happy and valued staff will work better and are less likely to be ill than their more neglected colleagues.)

Iona, an experienced teacher, finds it helpful when her headteacher ensures that, as far as possible, staff have plenty of advance notice of forthcoming events.

It's good because the head tries to give us plenty of warning about things so we can plan ahead.

Some headteachers try to act as a buffer between the outside world and their staff. This is not always straightforward, as Edna and Victoria explain,

When the SATS came, I thought, 'Do I show it to them straight away or do I . . .' and in the end I just said, 'The SATS have come; when you want them, they're in my room'. But all the time you're thinking, 'Do I put a bit more pressure on or is this the time to do it or not?'

I can remember trying to find a time when I could talk to a teacher about leading a staff development day. It was during the December term and I was thinking, 'Well, Christmas is pretty much on their plates; I won't talk to this teacher at this particular moment because I know if she's feeling uptight about this . . .'. Well, there was a lot of staff sickness, including this teacher, and I thought, 'Well, I'll wait a bit, until she's feeling better.' But time marched on and it wasn't until three weeks before the event that I wanted her to perform that I was actually able to have a word with her.

The same heads, and many of their colleagues, also feel that it is important to consult with their staff whenever appropriate and possible. Kate finds that such an approach can be very time consuming but that, in the long run, it is well worth the effort.

If you want to do everything thoroughly, negotiating with governors, involving consultation with the staff etc., and evolving a policy, and if it's going to be a worthwhile thing, it takes time, which means you can only do one or two things a term or year, which means there are a whole host of areas you haven't touched on.

How to create a working democracy when the headteacher is often ultimately responsible is by no means easy. Kate felt that there may have been a problem at her previous school because the head was almost too democratic.

When I was a deputy at the other school, I think one of the problems was that we'd created such a kind of democratic situation that everyone felt that their voice was important therefore they didn't really see that the head actually had the ultimate say. I think everybody has got to have a voice, has got to be listened to and got to be heard, and then you've got to come to a consensus, and as yet, at the school I'm at, I haven't been in a situation where I feel that we haven't all been fairly well behind the decisions that have been made. I'm not saying we haven't experienced conflict along the way in discussions and raised issues and disagreed with each other, but when we finally come to the decision, generally speaking, we are pretty well behind it.

Harriet has tried to evolve what might be considered a democratic leadership style,

At the end of the day we need all these policy statements and, although meetings are a burden, it's a help to share the load of the decision making. Although I might be leading the decisions — 'I would recommend you do this,' or, 'I suggest you do this or this' — it helps to know that there are other people involved in actually coming to that decision; that you've thought about it together and come to a mutual agreement.

This approach is greatly appreciated by her staff, one of whom enthuses,

At staff meetings now, if someone says, 'We'll do so-and-so and so-and-so,' it's okay to say 'That's not a democratic decision,' and it's great.

Figure 5.1: *Everybody has got to have a voice*

Unfortunately staff in other schools are not so lucky.

> She [the headteacher] doesn't want to be told by anyone else.
> She wants to do everything her way.

The issues of change and control will be taken up again in Chapter 7. Although a related topic, however, it seemed more appropriate to consider one-to-one interactions between headteachers and individual members of their staff in this chapter.

From my discussions, it seems that — apart from the usual exchanges — headteachers find themselves talking to a teacher specifically for one of three main reasons: to encourage staff development, to resolve a conflict, or to praise them. None of these situations is necessarily straightforward.

Teachers, it seems, can find it hard to cope with exchanges with senior staff for a variety of reasons. Broadly speaking, these may be classified in terms of the general atmosphere, personality traits and the way in which potentially sensitive issues are handled. Here, four teachers in different schools describe aspects of the general ethos of their situations which make them feel on edge. In his previous school Steve,

> . . . just found people running around always in a panic. There was always a situation. You were getting stress from the children and from senior colleagues. You didn't have room to relax.

Brenda thinks that her headteacher is very concerned with everyone keeping up appearances.

> Possibly a headteacher could, in theory, perform the role of counsellor if you didn't have to worry about forever trying to impress.

While Gary appreciates that the amount of stress his headteacher experiences must fluctuate, he says,

> It can be very difficult because she's somebody who is not always the same . . . She's not always open to what is being said and you can't always predict her moods.

And Marianne permanently feels on the defensive because,

> . . . there is just so much to cover. I can't possibly do it all in the depth I would like.

In part, I suspect, Marianne's views reveal aspects of the school's concern to cover the National Curriculum but, in part, they reveal something about her. Here some other teachers discuss facets of themselves that can make interactions with their headteachers uncomfortable.

> If I'm really honest, I am rather scared of the idea of going on a course. I know I look confident but I'm not at all and everyone always seems to know so much more than me.

> I would never, ever talk to any headteacher — however kind they were — about a problem I had because that would be admitting defeat, you see.

> I'm not very good at coping with criticism. Unless I feel it's justified. Otherwise I'm inclined to put up a bit of a defensive smoke-screen.

And, on a more positive note,

> Sometimes I chat to Susan [the headteacher] on the phone and she says, 'Oh, you're wonderful. You're great.' And sometimes I find it quite hard to take that because I've not had it before.

Two of the teachers I worked with recognized that their headteachers could, legitimately, play a role in their staff's development. They frequently found, however, that the heads concerned were less than tactful in their approach.

> I think I do feel the head is still rather threatening. I noticed that she came in today and was talking to a boy in my class and asking some questions about the reading scheme, and he couldn't answer her questions. She'd asked him related things that we'd covered well before Christmas so I wasn't surprised in a sense that he couldn't answer what she was asking. But I was conscious that she was asking questions and was perhaps making a judgment about what I was teaching or how well I taught it, because he couldn't answer her questions.

> Sometimes it feels like the headteacher has taken the place of a class teacher and I'm a child at school again.

Given that headteachers do hold a responsible position and generally are concerned about the morale and development of their staff, what can they do to avoid some of the pitfalls described above? The following suggestions from headteachers, their staff and the literature may be easy to say but they are only possible approaches and difficult ones at that!

> We start from the premise that self-awareness is a necessary starting point for encouraging and facilitating the development of others. (Powell and Solity, 1990, p.115)

As a headteacher, it certainly seems valuable to try to understand yourself as a person and consider your strengths, weaknesses and how you react to praise and criticism. Added to this is your professional persona which is not value-free. Harriet explains,

> I see everybody on an equal footing as myself but my role doesn't put me on an equal footing in other people's eyes.

Being realistic about your staff's assets, limitations and possible reactions can also prove a real bonus. More specifically, for example, having explored what stresses you, reflect on your staff as individuals, bearing in mind that,

> . . . stress is different for everybody and there are probably things that you find difficult that other people would say, 'What on earth do you find that difficult for?'

And the fact that most teachers seem to,

> . . . take the job very personally. I can't put my job there and my person here and say, 'Okay, they are criticizing me as a teacher.' I take it very personally because you put so much into your teaching. It's an intensely personal thing.

Moreover, that the feeling of,

> . . . failure is incredibly stressful. I'm thinking about people whom I've counselled who have been failing and I've seen the stress in them and actually sharing that with them is hard.

It also helps if you can trust your teachers as professionals and treat them as such. Certainly they will sometimes do things that you might not necessarily agree with but, in all honesty, will they do any major damage if they do not follow your advice and philosophy? If the answer is yes, then you might seriously wish to consider tackling the situation at the grass-roots level rather than constantly undermining the individual and almost certainly making what you consider a less than satisfactory performance even worse. Olive admits that she may not be a wonderful teacher but she is in no doubt that,

> It's nice to feel that you're trusted as a grown-up to make sensible decisions about things.

And Paula approves of Mrs V's strategy,

> The head is usually very good at praising when you deserve it and perhaps keeping quiet when you don't.

And finally on this issue, perhaps many people reading this will identify with these comments by two teachers.

> I think I get more stressed simply because I am very hard on myself. I'm my own worst enemy. I can never actually see that I do any good. I can only ever see all the things I don't do.

> I've got a post of responsibility which worries me a bit because I feel I'm not doing what I should be doing, that I'm failing. I'm told I'm not but you always worry that you are not living up to people's expectations.

Praise can indeed be hard to accept but — and I am still working on this myself — we have to learn to take it at face value and respond appropriately. Saying, 'Oh, it was nothing,' after all suggests that the complimenter has little idea of what's what. In contrast, replying, 'Thank you. I was pleased with it myself,' is, I am told, mutually beneficial.

Concluding Remarks

This is a long chapter which covers a range of important and sensitive issues. For me the underlying conclusions are that we are all human and — unless we have definite evidence to the contrary — we are all professionals endeavouring to do our jobs to the best of our ability. By implication this means that we all — even headteachers — need praise and reassurance from time to time and, every once in a while, we need to be told when it is time to stop. Headteachers Harriet and Edna certainly appreciate it when their staff make such gestures.

And as I've got confirmation that perhaps I am quite good at some things so my confidence has been boosted.

I think if they find me looking very tired and stressed either the deputy or somebody will say to me, 'Come on, what's the matter?' So there are people in school, I think, who watch me.

And finally, two tributes to headteachers who seem to be getting it right.

She did absolutely the right thing when I rushed in at nine o'clock in a panic after my car had broken down on the way to school and she smiled and said, 'Oh, it's lovely to see you'.

It's like working with your mum. I love it. It's great. It's a lot calmer than my last school. First name terms and actually just talking to people on a professional level. Every time you talk to the head you don't think the world's falling apart again. It's just a nice relaxed atmosphere.

Summary

- Being a senior member of staff is not always easy!
- Neither a new headteacher nor his/her staff should underestimate the time, sensitivity and effort it can take to acclimatize to one another.
- Deputy headteachers sometimes feel that they have demands on their time and attention coming from all directions which can make it difficult for them to achieve the high standards they set themselves.
- It is vitally important to develop good working relationships and a happy atmosphere within a school.
- Many headteachers find the following particularly stressful:- paperwork, relationships with staff, parents, governors, the media, school budgets, lack of time, overload, the unpredictability of the job, almost non-stop decision-making, the burden

of continual responsibility and the assumptions others have of their role.

- Headteacher stress can be reduced through good planning, appropriate delegation, effective communication, lists, prioritizing, postponing less essential work, finding a suitable place to work, standing back, viewing things in perspective and enjoying a visit to a reception class!
- With observation, imagination and thought there are a variety ways in which headteachers and their staff may ease one another's professional burden.
- Unless you have evidence to the contrary, assume everyone is working to the best of their ability!
- We *all* need praise and reassurance from time to time.

Further Reading and References

COOPER, C. and KELLY, M. (1993) 'Occupational stress in headteachers: A national UK study', *British Journal of Educational Psychology*, **63**, pp.130–43.
EVERTSON, C.M. and HARRIS, A.H. (1992) 'What we know about managing classrooms', *Educational Leadership*, **49**, pp.74–8.
FONTANA, D. (1989) *Managing Stress*, Leicester and London, The British Psychological Society in association with Routledge.
POWELL M. and SOLITY J. (1990) *Teachers in Control*, London, Routledge.

Another useful book is:

CRAIG, I. (ed.) (1987) *Primary School Management in Action*, Harlow, Longman.

6   The Challenges of Time

A job is defined by hours and a profession isn't: you do the job
until it's done. (Helena)

Time — or rather the lack of it — is the bane of my life. Of all the
stresses and strains the teachers discussed, the issue of time was the
only one they all mentioned without exception. There is no doubt
about it: being a teacher (and here I include headteachers!) takes considerable time.

It would be naive and wrong of me to present this chapter as the
answer to all your problems as far as time is concerned. That would be
impossible. I hope, however, it will raise some interesting questions
and include a range of thoughts and ideas for you to consider. You
might, of course, have read numerous books on general time management and feel that I can have nothing more to offer. You might well be
right, but I would argue that teaching is a particular case which presents
its own specific difficulties and dilemmas.

'The Race is On'

I've started to get up half-past six instead of quarter to seven but
even then, I don't think it matters what time you get up, you
adjust your pace accordingly and I'm still in a rush.

As soon as the children are in it's 'go' until quarter past three.

You always feel as though you're chasing your tail.

Lunchtime is from 12 till one and I often find myself thinking,
'Oh, crumbs, it's quarter to one and I haven't eaten yet,' and
then I have to rush around and have something quickly.

I've tried taking a quarter of an hour to myself in my room after
lunch. It worked for a while but then it became counter-
productive because I was sitting there thinking, 'I ought to be
getting on with something'.

Well, I've got a senior midday supervisor so officially I think I can go and leave her in charge. I find if I have to go down to the next village to go to the bank or something, you tend to drive very fast because your head is . . . You're sort of driving along like this . . . As I discovered, you get done for speeding!

I'm conscious that I would like to have a walk every day but it gets pushed out because of school work.

I get very resentful about the amount of time it takes up.

If I have meetings, then fine: I'm awake, alert and nerves carry you through. But if I'm at home, once I've eaten my meal I will settle down to watch the video that I missed because I was at a meeting, and fall asleep.

I used to go to evening classes and I find that either there isn't time or I'm just too tired.

You need time to relax. You need to unwind. But then you're thinking that if you do too much of that you've lost the time to do what you're worrying about and you create another stress there.

I'm only 30 and yet a lot of nights I end up in bed by half-past eight.

Sometimes I could really sleep on a linen line.

I was actually making myself very tired and exhausted with the long hours.

I had three days off recently and I was in a lot of pain but I still felt guilty.

It tends to be the case that you actually collapse at the end of a term and invariably you're ill over a holiday or half-term.

It's only in the summer holidays that you actually switch off from it.

An outsider reading the above perhaps might be forgiven for thinking that I was making my data up, despite my reassurances that the remarks were taken directly from the teachers, deputies and headteachers to whom I spoke. In contrast, I suspect, practitioners will be able to identify with some — if not most — of them only too well.

- Is it a necessary part of the job that so many should feel this way?
- How do such time pressures affect one's performance as a teacher?
- What are the effects on others — such as the pupils — around you in school?
- Does it influence your home life and the quality of your life in general?
- Could you make better use of your time?

By standing back and trying to view yourself and your own situation more objectively, I hope you will gain some insights which may ease your time pressures and give you pause for thought.

Time to Understand: You as a Human Being

There seems little doubt that teachers lead what might be described as rather 'unnatural lives'. Victoria expresses it thus,

Teachers live this rather strange lifestyle of being intensely busy and then having holiday periods when they actually recharge their batteries and collapse.

There are other professions — such as medicine — which are similar, but the majority seem to be as Lillian's former job,

I worked as an administrator before. It was stressful but I could leave it at the end of the time and I didn't have to worry about it at night-time or weekends ever!

A recurrent theme in this book is that there is never enough time for a teacher, deputy or head to do all that there is to be done. You could almost call it a fact. It is also true — unless I have been very badly misled! — that teachers (and here I include deputies and heads) are human beings with basic needs to eat, sleep and to go to the lavatory. Moreover, if they are to perform at their best, it is crucial that they take time to relax. Indeed Kirsta is clear,

> One of the most important points to remember is that you should
> schedule your leisure activities as carefully as your work. (1986,
> p.75)

As human beings, we all have our own innate body rhythms which
— if we can work with them rather than against them — can help us
live our lives more effectively. Probably the best known of these rhythms
is the circadian — or 24-hour — cycle. Apparently, 'all living organ-
isms, from cabbages to kings, are geared to this circadian rhythm,'
(Norfolk, 1985, p.120). It is generally thought that these rhythms are
inherited and cannot easily be changed. Thus, as a first step, it is important to recognize whether you are a lark or an owl.

> The owls are slow to get going in the morning, but function
> well at night. The larks wake easily, do their best work in the
> morning, but tire soon after lunch and need to retire early to
> bed. (Norfolk, 1985, p.121)

Part of the problem of being a teacher is that many of us try to
interfere with our circadian rhythms. We go to bed early during the
week, for example, and then we expect to stay up till all hours at the
weekend. Be we a lark or an owl, such a lifestyle cannot be done
without paying a price. (That, as I have observed, might include falling
asleep at a dinner party!) As a teacher you have little option but to rise
early but, if you are an owl, perhaps you can make getting up as gentle
and unhassled as possible and leave any essential rushing around until
later in the day if you can.

Before moving on to consider teaching specifically, it is also important that you stand back and try to identify the basic needs in your
life. By these I do not mean £1,000,000 or an ideal partner who is
totally devoted to you and will carry out your every whim. What, and
how much, you require of any one thing will entirely depend on you
as an individual but, in compiling your list, you would probably do
well to consider the following.

- How much sleep do you need? Some people, I understand,
  only require 3–4 hours a night but, realistically, how long do
  you need to feel rested in the morning? Do you get and/or
  could you rearrange things so that you go to bed and get up
  at approximately the same time each day?
- Are you a camel or do you need feeding and watering at frequent intervals? If the latter, take note and try to incorporate

appropriate snacks into your day so that you can make the best use of your time even when your blood sugar is relatively low (e.g., perhaps just before lunch).

- Do you take sufficient time to relax and do you do so effectively? More will be said about this below.
- How much exercise do you take? Is it enough? Is it enjoyable? If not, it probably is not time well spent as the disadvantages may be outweighing the benefits.
- Do you have sufficient solitude? To my mind solitude is remarkably underrated. It is not always easy to come by and, to some, it may seem very threatening. But it is not at all the same as loneliness and it can be incredibly rejuvenating. Kirsta (1986) advocates,

> . . . the more time you spend with other people, the more important it is to keep some time to spend on your own. (1986, p.77)

Time to Understand: You as a Teacher

Understanding yourself as a human being may be all very well — indeed, as will be discussed in Chapter 8, it is essential — but what can you as a teacher do to make better use of your time? Despite (or perhaps because of?) the worries about time management, the teachers came up with a surprising number of suggestions which they found effective. No one person used them all but perhaps, if one does, life would be less dominated by the clock.

Personal Observation

Observe, firstly, how you spend your time; secondly, what creates stress-related time pressures for you; and finally, note the effects these have on you and those around you. So, how do you spend your time? Do you waste it? Do you enjoy it? And, as will be discussed later in this chapter, do you use it efficiently? Taking the second matter — how time creates stress for you — Julie finds,

> I don't always sleep well because I am afraid I'm going to miss the alarm, oversleep and be late for school. Someone suggested I use two alarms, so I must try that.

Regarding the third focus of observation — the effect on others — Gordon notes,

> I don't like the time pressure. I find that quite stressful. And it works through to the children and makes them tense too, I think. When I notice that, I try to do something about it like change the pace of things a little bit.

Listing, Prioritizing, Grouping, Discarding

Making lists can also save time for a number of reasons. One, quite simply, is that it relieves the brain of having to remember so much, providing you with better quality thinking time (see also Chapter 5). Incidentally, should something occur to you late at night, try not to turn on your bedside light as this is likely to trick your eyes into thinking it is daytime, making it harder to get to sleep. Perhaps you could invest in a small torch or write in the dark or even kick a shoe (or some such object) into the middle of the room as a reminder!

Effective list-making can help you *prioritize, group or discard jobs* as appropriate. Graham finds that,

> If I put the children's agenda first and it works well, then it frees me to follow my agenda, and I do it sometimes by making the children aware of what my agenda is so that they cooperate. 'I need to be doing this. I'm asking you to do this. I'm asking you to work without me to free me to do whatever it is that I need to do in the classroom.'

Katrina tends to place high priority on jobs which could grow if not attended to sooner rather than later. She advises,

> Don't let things build up. Try and keep on top of things as they actually happen.

Grouping jobs together often allows for greater efficiency. For example, rather than running up and down the school doing one job here and another there, you can save time by doing all the errands situated at one end of the building before tackling tasks located elsewhere.

Discarding jobs may, to some, seem like sacrilege. Nevertheless some headteachers do it (see Chapter 5) and Donald Norfolk argues,

The simplest way to preserve your store of energy is to prevent other people wasting it. (1985, p.145)

If you are worried about not taking on a particular task, you might like to find out why you were asked to tackle it in the first place. This, in itself, may take a little time but it might give you peace of mind and make any discarding easier in the future. Headteacher Fred carried out just such an investigation.

I asked County Hall, 'Who uses the information on this form?' Months later I got the reply, 'Nobody'. It was obviously information that at one stage somebody had wanted — the Parish or someone — and it had gone on one year and then never been removed from the form.

Planning

Another way to look at these activities is to *plan effectively*. Rowland and Birkett suggest,

Some people would argue that this [i.e., preparation] contributes to at least 90 per cent of all teachers' success rates. Good preparation will give you confidence. (1992, p.44)

Victoria, a headteacher, uses a system which she finds very effective.

Before I leave work every night I map out the next day. I have a sheet of A4 which my secretary has designed for me, and I map out all the appointments and the timetable, all the people I've got to ring, staff I want to contact, as well as a section for long-term plans or things that I want to think about.

A copy has been set out in figure 6.1 and, although it would need some modification, I suspect it could also be a valuable tool for teachers and deputies. However good your planning, try not to be too frustrated when attacked by 'time bandits' as described by Donald (p.93 of Chapter 5): in a busy school it is inevitable that you will be interrupted and your plans will go by the board now and again. When they do, perhaps you need to ask yourself, 'Does it *really* matter?' Ninety-nine times out of a hundred, I suspect, a delay will make little difference.

Schools are curious learning environments. If you think about it, is

Daily Log Sheet

Date ....

Timetable

9.00

9.30

10.20   Assembly

11.00

11.30

12.00

12.30

1.00

1.30

2.00

2.30

3.00

Figure 6.1:   Victoria's planning sheet

it not a little bizarre that many people imagine that every child in a class — particularly if they are upper primary or beyond — will learn in bite-size units generally called 'periods'? Not only that, but we, as teachers, work up their interest and then, when we have got them going, we seem to expect them to switch from one subject to the next in a couple of minutes as a bell, or its equivalent, dictates.

A couple of strategies were suggested if you *are* bound by such a regime (see below). Brenda felt very stressed,

> . . . working to the clock all day long . . . All the time you've got to watch the clock.

It was then suggested that she sets a small alarm for 5–10 minutes before the end of every lesson so that she can *concentrate on teaching* and both she and her pupils have a short time to gather their thoughts, summarize key points if necessary, and tidy their things away.

Concentration and Relaxation

If we are honest, even the most disciplined of us cannot concentrate for long periods of time without a break. The younger the child, the shorter this time seems to be. (Though, have you ever watched a 5 year old watch their favourite television programme?) If one day you are feeling particularly driven by time, such that you and your pupils are finding it hard to focus on the lesson in hand, you might all like to try to *relax during the session* as Nina describes.

> I've got several relaxation tapes that I actually use in class with the children as well, for us to have just five minutes' peace.

Another similar technique is to stop what you are doing and suggest everyone does a few exercises together. This — say in the form of 'Simon says' — tends to work well with younger children and usually settles them down. I am not sure it would be welcomed by their older brothers and sisters though!

Modifying the Timetable

The younger your pupils the more likely you are to be able to *modify the timetable* to suit your and the children's needs. Thus, for example, if a maths investigation is going particularly well it is often possible to let the children continue, taking the entire morning if necessary. This, of course, may leave you less time to cover English on that particular day, but surely that can be shunted to another day or another week even? It could also be argued that, by becoming absorbed in one particular activity, one is in grave danger of falling behind in your curriculum coverage. I can appreciate the point but — and I am in no position to make judgments here — it might be worth considering whether you wish to encourage your pupils to understand the content of their lessons or you wish to provide them with a broader sweep of information. Maybe you endeavour to opt for a combination of the two. (In passing, the issue is not only complicated by the constraints of your school's systems but by other factors relating to classroom processes: see Desforges and Cockburn (1987) listed at the end of the chapter.)

Before moving on, I personally find that I generally save time if I complete one job before starting another. This, obviously, is not always possible, especially in a busy school environment but, when you think about it, one can spend quite a bit of time 'thinking oneself back into a task' that has had to be abandoned previously.

Making Time to Relax

Both teachers and management experts often recommend that one *takes time to relax* during the working day. This, most practitioners seem to find incredibly hard to do for a variety of reasons, too much to do being top of the list! Donald Norfolk, however, cites an interesting study.

> When a team of physiologists studied the work patterns of a group of factory workers in Dortmund, West Germany they found that the men took rest pauses whenever they were needed but concealed them from their foremen by indulging in some form of masking activity, such as idly polishing their machines. In one factory it was found that these unauthorized breaks took up to 11 per cent of the working day. Since there was no way in which they could be curbed, the firm decided to accept them as inevitable and made the bold experiment of introducing official rest pauses of five minutes at the end of every hour's work. Once this scheme was instigated the hidden breaks disappeared, fatigue was lessened, and production rose by 13 per cent. (1985, p.116)

Now, I am not suggesting that you are concealing anything, nor am I saying that your school should immediately institute five-minute breaks every hour (though it might be a good idea!) but I think the points about fatigue and efficiency are worth noting.

Being Ill

One thing many of the teachers I spoke to found extremely difficult was taking time off when they were ill.

> If I'm sick at any time I feel guilty and then there's an added stress when I get back because I want to catch up.

> Time off is a double-edged sword. I once had to take two-and-a-half weeks off and during that time the children had a number of different teachers, and when I came back they were off the ceiling. It was awful.

I certainly empathize but, if we are strictly honest, are any of us doing ourselves, our colleagues or our pupils any good when we struggle in to work feeling definitely under the weather? Whether we like it or not, I strongly suspect we can make better use of everyone's time if we *take a couple of days off* when the symptoms show they mean business rather than crawling in until we pass our germs on to all and sundry and really go down with something serious.

Delegation

In Chapters 3 and 5 I discussed how one might delegate tasks in school. I also think that it is important that we *delegate* some jobs at home too. Certainly if one has a family it is perfectly in order to expect all those who can talk — babies may be excused — to help you out. Whatever your domestic circumstances I, and several of the teachers, can certainly recommend your finding a good cleaner. The right person can usually do an amazing amount in 2–3 hours per week and they are unlikely to break the bank. They can certainly save you time and help lighten your mood.

> I do have a cleaning lady so I don't clean. That's been a tremendous boon because I used to get very stroppy about having to spend the whole weekend cleaning the house.

Housework I don't worry about because I have somebody in to do it now. I insisted upon that, and it's lovely to walk into a house — it gives you a real lift when it smells nice and clean.

A word of warning though: good cleaners can be hard to come by and it seems to be best to go on personal recommendation. Perhaps one of the school's cleaners might be interested or perhaps a colleague has already found someone who would be happy to take on some extra hours.

Time to Work

Starting and stopping working at home can often be difficult. Victoria explains her technique of *setting aside time to work*.

I suppose, to summarize, it's setting yourself deadlines. 'I will work up until such-and-such a time.' I do that at the weekend; it helps me to actually get down to it because otherwise I will find some washing that desperately needs to be done, or the ironing, you know: I simply can't look at this unironed shirt any longer. So I will say to myself, well, I will work between 4 and 5 and then I will stop.

Knowing when to stop not only stops you wasting your time when you could be doing something more worthwhile, but it also gives you an important break from the job (see Chapter 8).

You try not to be too emotional about it. You just try and cut yourself off. It's a pretty hard thing to do though, because it [the job] does stay with you. (brackets added)

I have to fight the temptation to constantly work my way through the whole weekend as well as the week, and my days will be 11, 12 hours long for two or three days of the week with no break, not even a lunch break. And that's — you have to step back sometimes and say, 'Hang on a minute. You've got to get this sorted out.'

Setting Limits

A variation of this is to *set yourself limits*. These might be defined in terms of time or events.

I think you have to discipline yourself to say — as I have done
— 'Right, I'm not working Friday nights. I will start work Sunday nights.' I think that that's very important, to feel that you
can have that time and not feel 'I shouldn't be doing this,' but
to feel, 'No, this is my time'.

I rarely work after I've eaten at night. So if I have got something
to do I'll do it and then eat. So then I can switch off with a clear
conscience.

An absorbing hobby which — ideally — you do on a regular basis
can prove a major asset,

I have an outside interest in sailing and I find total relaxation
wrestling with a boat, especially when it is blowing a hooley
and you are about to be thrown into the water.

Another valuable strategy is to put 'me' time in your diary which
'should be as precious as a meeting'. Rachel is quite clear about it,

You've got to have space for yourself. You've got to build in —
hopefully every day but that's not always possible — time when
you can say, 'This is my time. This is for me and nobody's going
to encroach on it.'

Apart from such time being enjoyable (hopefully!) it will almost certainly save you time in the long run. Kate's experience has shown her
that she is right when she says,

Make sure that you give yourself time. You've actually got to
say, 'In order to do this job well, I've actually got to have some
time to myself.'

For a whole host of reasons (some of which will be discussed in
Chapter 8) your personal life should not be neglected but, from a time
and efficiency point of view, Donald explains,

If things are not working well domestically, I think that shouldn't
be underestimated. I think you can very often handle a difficult
situation at work, or maybe even two or three difficult situations
at work, as long as things are running smoothly at home. You
can handle a difficult situation at home as long as things are

running smoothly at work, but I think just on the odd occasion, particularly because of one or two features of life over the last two or three years — if you have a serious illness, one of your own children is unhappy at school themselves, a bill or two that are difficult to pay, any one of those things (and I mean, most teachers I know have those sort of problems) — that, coupled with two or three situations at work, and you're beginning to wobble, which makes the job extremely difficult to do effectively.

Standing Back

Most people, when they are stressed, seem to spend a lot of time fretting rather than being constructive. A further piece of advice from the teachers is to *stand back* from time to time.

> I think holidays are really important. You should get away — right away — and give yourself time to get it all in perspective, because you can get so submerged in it all that it's difficult to see the wood for the trees.

And Laura makes a radical suggestion based on experience,

> The Christmas before last we went to Germany for the whole two weeks, leaving the day after school broke up and returning the day before school started, and I was in a real state about, 'I can't do this. I've got to go into school. I've got to get ready. I can't possibly do it.' And my husband, Tim, said, 'Well, we're doing it otherwise we can't get on a flight.' And we did it and it turned out to be the best thing for me, I think. A complete break, and I felt as if I'd been away a lot longer than two weeks. It was brilliant.

Summary

In conclusion, there will nearly always be too much for you to do, but be kind to yourself and take Harriet's advice,

> Do what you can. Forget the rest. Because you can only do so much. If you haven't done it, you haven't done it.

Remembering that,

> It's easy to do and say that when you're not tired and you're not overloaded. But a combination of circumstances and a lot of events coming in crowding out the time you've set aside for yourself, and you are tired: it's then it gets out of proportion.

Figure 6.2: A summary of practitioners' suggestions to make better use of time

Further Reading and References

There are numerous books on time management, some of which are likely to be more realistic for you than others given the constraints under which you work. A recent and accessible volume is:

FONTANA, D. (1993) *Managing Time*, Leicester, BPS Books.

Also of interest might be:

CAMPBELL, R.J., EVANS, L., ST. J. NEILL, S.R. and PACKWOOD, A. (1993) *The Use and Management of Infant Teachers' Time*, Stoke-on-Trent, Trentham Books.

The books mentioned in the text are also helpful for a variety of reasons, as their titles suggest.

DESFORGES, C. and COCKBURN, A.D. (1987) *Understanding the First School Mathematics Teacher*, London, Falmer Press.
KIRSTA, A. (1986) *The Book of Stress Survival*, London, Gaia Books.
NORFOLK, D. (1985) *Farewell to Fatigue*, London, Pan Books.
ROWLAND, V. and BIRKETT, K. (1992) *Personal Effectiveness for Teachers*, Hemel Hempstead, Simon and Schuster Education.

7   Change and Control

The changes over the last few years in education have been phenomenal. Although much can be said about those changes (see below), this chapter is not about them *per se*. Rather it will endeavour to paint a broader picture of change and, to a lesser extent, the nature of control as it relates to change.

All manner of changes affect our lives: life changes, seasonal changes, job changes, curriculum changes, class changes and so on and so forth. Some are self-initiated. Others are not. Some may be easy. Others less so. Some you may agree with. Others you may not. Many people — and some of the teachers I spoke to were no exception — find change stressful.

> I don't like changes of any sort.

> I think we're going through a very big change at the moment and change is always stressful, isn't it?

> Getting to grips with something new is always stressful.

Others seem to view it as a necessary part of their professional life.

> I used to find change difficult to cope with but I think I actually like change . . . I can't stand it if things stay the same.

> I believe that if you're not changing then you've had it really. You've become complacent and you're not moving on and you're not sort of reflecting on what you're doing.

Unfortunately, sometimes such people did not always appreciate the complexities and anxieties people experience when the notion of change is introduced. Indeed their lack of sympathy can further exacerbate the problem.

Some Thoughts on Why Change can be Stressful

Whether you are the initiator of the change or not (see below) there seem to be five concerns which may apply to change:

- the risk
- your commitment
- the effect on your performance
- the time
- the effect on others.

(As I write I am thinking mainly of professional change but I suspect these considerations could equally well relate to other changes in your life.)

The Risk

Making changes can be risky as,

> In such a complex enterprise as the promotion of education innovation, which is so much influenced by its own particular setting and by the participants, no guarantees of success . . . can be offered. (Nicholls, 1983, p.1)

This can seem particularly true when you have got everything as you want it and someone comes along and insists that you make a change. And, if you think about it, it is not simply chance that things are the way they are in your classroom, for I suspect that there is a lot of truth in Greeno's suggestion that,

> . . . the nature of the concepts and skills to be acquired [in school] has been shaped by a process of evolution in which materials that cannot be learned by most students [i.e., pupils] and methods of instruction that are patently unsuccessful have been eliminated over the years. (1980, p.726) (brackets added)

That is not to say that it is *not* possible to change classroom practice but simply that suggestions that fit in with 'current classroom procedures and . . . not cause major disruptions' (Feiman-Nemser and Loden, 1986, p.516) are more likely to succeed. Moreover it is important to remember that '. . . at some level . . . schools are properly conservative' (Rudduck,

1991, p.28): it would be irresponsible suddenly to risk a generation's education by turning everything on its head.

Your Commitment

Perhaps not surprisingly if you are committed to making a change your chances of success will increase: you are more likely to make more effort and attempt to overcome obstacles. If you are tentative you may be more half-hearted in your efforts. You may be even less enthusiastic if the change has been imposed on you and, rather than commitment, you feel resentment over what might seem a blatant lack of appreciation of all your past efforts.

The Effect on Your Performance

Whatever kind of changes you endeavour to make, it is as well to appreciate that other aspects of your performance may be affected. By way of analogy: you may have perfected your golf swing but as soon as you introduce a ball your swing may temporarily go to pot. So, for example, you may find that when trying out a new questioning technique your discipline is not up to its usual high standard. Recognizing this, you may be able to stave off the depression and demoralization that some experience with change.

Related to this is the problem that can arise when you are asked to add something new to the curriculum. A clear case was when the science curriculum rapidly expanded with the introducion of the National Curriculum. Such an addition inevitably took up teaching time and yet people wondered why standards were not consistently maintained in other subject areas!

The Time

Effective change takes time. Indeed William Shreshly and Mac Bernd (1992) go so far as to suggest that major school reforms can take up to ten years! That may be longer than we need to allow for for most of our purposes, but nevertheless it is an important factor to consider. This is especially true when a change may initiate the 'Hawthorne Effect'. This is a term commonly used in psychology when something temporarily changes (usually for the better) simply as a result of *a* change, not as a result of *the* change. In such cases, when the novelty of change wears off, things revert to as they were before the change. In other words, do not open the champagne until you have tested whether the effects of your change on pupils is only transitory!

The Effect on Others

Any changes you try to make will almost certainly have some impact on your pupils and possibly other members of staff. There may be no problem and they may well greet your new approach with enthusiasm and glee! On the other hand, children and teachers alike are often fairly conservative and familiar routines provide them with security: they know what to do and they can get on and do it without too much worry and hassle. Introduce something new, however, and it can be quite unsettling — What are we to do? What does the teacher want? Will I get it wrong? I don't understand! The result may be that — contrary to your expectations — there is some resistance to your new, 'improved' style and, indeed, you may see some similarities to your own reactions as discussed in the next section on imposed change.

Potential Problems with Imposed Change

When you try to institute changes yourself the experience can often be exciting and challenging. Problems can arise, however, if the idea comes from other staff, your headteacher or someone else altogether. Cynically, Nick Yapp suggested that,

> Education is like Ballroom Dancing — you're always moving to somebody else's tune and you're usually going in circles. (1987, p.34)

Apart from the issues discussed above, there seem to be three main factors which influence the likely success of externally imposed suggestions. The first is *your philosophical attitude towards it*: do you resent the idea or are you wholeheartedly behind it? Olive and Gordon describe their reactions to recent changes in their respective schools.

> I feel quite a lot of pressure from the legislation from the Department for Education. I feel that we're asked to do a lot of things which I personally deem to be irrelevant for the needs of my children, and I find that stressful.

I have to go along with it because that's what everyone else is adopting. Other people don't seem to see a problem. So, I go along with it but I haven't fundamentally changed my opinions, so that just leads to a little conflict.

Ulla also feels saddened to find herself frustrated by some imposed changes, as she explains in this short interview.

> *Ulla:* And I must admit I spend more of my time on language than I do on anything else, because I believe that if they can't read then you're causing enormous problems for people later on, and there's just too much to teach.
>
> *Anne:* So you are following your own philosophy bearing in mind the National Curriculum demands?
>
> *Ulla:* And that's stressful as well, isn't it, because you've got what you believe is right and also the fact that there's this exterior thing that's been imposed upon you that you've got to take into account as well that you may not necessarily believe in.
>
> *Anne:* It's getting in the way?
>
> *Ulla:* Mm. And it really does, for me. It really has taken away a lot of the pleasure. It seems like a chore where you've got to do this, we've got to jump over that hurdle, and the fact that things change so quickly.

The second factor which might influence success is *your understanding of the proposed change.* This, I hasten to add, is not intended as a veiled insult to your intelligence! Quite simply: if someone else has an idea there is no way, unless it is incredibly simple, that you can fully appreciate the thinking behind it unless you can climb inside their head (figuratively speaking, of course!). A lack of understanding can lead to teachers becoming, '. . . mere executors (if not the executioners) of someone else's decision,' (Kamii, 1985, p.xiv). As Gordon points out, however, this lack of shared understanding does not necessarily lead to negative outcomes when the imposed change comes in the form of a new member of staff.

> I meant to write down new staff as being a cause of stress. It's quite stressful when new people come, in general because all the shared understandings go out of the window. You can spend a lot of time writing curriculum documents with colleagues. But as soon as somebody else comes in, that shared understanding

goes out of the window and it's not possible to initiate them into all the things that have been said previously, so the shared understanding gets diluted. But it's stimulating at the same time — they react differently and perhaps have new ideas.

And the third factor which is likely to affect the success of a suggested change is, quite simply, *reality*. Anita explains,

. . . you've got a lot of people sending you instructions from on high and telling you how it should be done, and you know you can't do it like that because they don't know what the real world's like in a school.

Feiman-Nemser and Loden make a similar point, which also echoes the thinking behind Greeno's remark made earlier,

Those who criticise teachers for maintaining this 'practicality ethic' may underestimate the added complications that flow from attempts to alter established practice and the degree to which current practices are highly adaptive to classroom realities. (1986, p.516)

When the suggestion of change induces such negative responses it can also create a feeling of having little control. Edna expresses it thus,

I think people are feeling they have less control of what's happening to them. Things have come from outside, from the DFE, that you have to take on board.

Moreover, Aileen feels that there is little option but to introduce changes imposed by the government, as you, '. . . have to be accountable for every little thing you do,' and you have the threat of an inspection hanging over you. Such a situation puts teachers in an odd predicament for, as Brenda explains,

We do have autonomy in our own classroom which is good. But we don't seem to have autonomy anywhere else. That's difficult.

This feeling of little control can also make one negative to the very idea of change.

I haven't been happy about the fact that the curriculum keeps changing. No, I'm not happy about things like that at all. That sort of worries me on a different sort of plane, perhaps. Perhaps that's a sort of general unhappiness: I think, that's not fair. Then I turn the radio on and I hear a fortnightly moan at the 'teachers this' and 'teachers that'. It comes up on a regular basis, doesn't it? 'Teachers are going to have to do this now,' and I think, 'What next?' and I half don't listen to it any more.

For a headteacher the issue of change can be particularly difficult because, as Kate says,

I am accountable. I am ultimately responsible for what happens inside this school and the stress I feel is trying to help the staff to get externally imposed changes into perspective and saying, 'Look, you've got to be reasonable about this,' and trying to support them and help them feel a bit more confident — so helping them cope with the stresses that they are feeling, at the same time as I know that I cannot comply with all that is being demanded of me from outside. So, yes, it's trying to marry the two. I don't want to put additional stress on the teachers. There are certain things that we have to do. There are certain things that I feel are justified and I feel will actually improve practice within the school and I can quite happily rationalize that. But the kinds of things that we're asked to do that I feel don't benefit the school don't benefit the children, and yet I know I've got to do, I find stressful.

On the more positive side, Victoria says that one of the reasons she likes being a headteacher is that it gives her the opportunity 'to influence and bring about change'.

The National Curriculum and Change

Before moving on to discuss suggestions for easing the negative aspects of change, I thought it important to have a short section on the National Curriculum and change. In part this is because the people I interviewed had so much to say on the matter. It also raises some interesting issues and — with luck — it might be seen as a piece of history rather than something some individuals perceive as an 'ongoing nightmare'.

Before she became a teacher, one of my interviewees observed the process as a governor, and described the teachers' experience thus,

> . . . it must feel like every time they scramble to their feet they have the rug pulled from under.

Here are some practitioners' thoughts on the matter.

> Things like technology changed before we even got it going.

> You just think you've become familiar with one set and then it changes and you have to re-learn a whole new set.

> I am aware that my knowledge of the National Curriculum is actually slipping and becoming outdated because it is changing so rapidly.

> Assessment is increasingly complex and changing. In my time at the school (3 years) there hasn't been a system that's up and working. We're always having to invent new systems.

> I quite agree with the National Curriculum, that there should be some standards that everyone is aiming to. I don't like the way they've gone about it at all. I think most teachers would say that's the biggest problem, the way it's just been piled on too quickly without any thought. I like the concept and I think it probably will get there eventually but after how many hundreds of millions of pounds, how much stress it's caused, how much time it's wasted, how many children have had to chop and change.

> I think the teachers are getting shell-shocked. I think they're at the stage where it doesn't matter what it is, but for goodness sake let's not have too much more. We can't do everything. They're obviously keener if it's school generated. But there isn't the enthusiasm that there used to be.

On a more positive note:

> The music National Curriculum has been good. It's widened our outlook and it's made us think very much more about what we're doing.

I mean, I think the National Curriculum and all that's implied has actually made me much more aware — I suppose I was too narrow in what I was doing. It's made me think about all the other areas that there are to do, to cover. I think they've gone too far. I think we cover too much, but it does stop you doing your favourite things over again.

And, of course, we have been told that there will be no changes to the National Curriculum in the next five years.

Strategies to Ease Innovations and Change

William Shreshly and Mac Bernd (1992) suggest that effective innovations require 'vision — a deep understanding of what exceptional schools can accomplish' (p.321); a real appreciation of all the relevant factors and time. I have no reason to doubt that but interestingly all the practitioners' suggestions were, in some way, related to imposed changes. Not all are compatible and your opinion of them may well depend on the position in which you find yourself.

The first is an implicit suggestion and involves *timing*. Nora was somewhat bewildered when the changes,

> . . . came thick and fast with the National Curriculum and a new headteacher on the scene.

Perhaps it would have been difficult to do very much about the onslaught of the National Curriculum. And, I suspect, it is only natural that a new head should want to make some changes. But perhaps she could have slowed down a little: the general point being that people can only cope with so many changes at one time.

The second suggestion was to *phase in changes*. Penny, an individual who says that she finds change threatening, very much appreciated her headteacher's understanding when she introduced a Real Book approach for,

> She told us we can give the children a choice from a reading scheme as well and that has helped us who are used to schemes.

It is not that Penny thinks change is necessarily a bad thing — most of the head's changes 'are for the better' — but she felt happier combining the old and the new until she was convinced that Real Books were an effective means of teaching her children.

Bill Laar and his colleagues believe that, 'Agreeing policies as a whole school is the foundation of effective teaching' (1989, p.4). And perhaps it is not surprising — especially given one of the recurring suggestions in this book — that the third policy is to, and I quote, '*Talk, talk, talk, talk, talk*'.

Providing an opportunity for plenty of talk opens up the possibility of several useful things happening. One of these is that colleagues can gain a shared understanding of what is required of them and how they might implement the proposed changes in a coherent and effective manner. Talking also enables people to learn — and possibly amend their ways — without having a spotlight put on them. Pauline explains how these two benefits came about at her school.

> We've discussed things and we've changed our ways in a lot of things, and haven't felt that we've been criticized; we've just got on and changed. Because it's all done in staff meetings, it does make that sort of thing easier, if we talk about things together, all of us, and then we know if we're doing something that doesn't really follow what we should be doing, and we can quietly go away and put ourselves right.

Talking also enables one to say 'one's piece'. Several of the teachers I spoke to said that, while they did not always agree with policies created and accepted by their colleagues, they invariably felt better for having stated their objections. Ulla suggests that more primary teachers should go one step further and tell the government what they think.

> I mean, you can't have a piece of evidence for everything I report on a child, and I think it's time for us actually to say, 'Come on, that's impossible, we can't do it. We're professionals, and I am saying I think this child is so-and-so, and I think that should be good enough.' The government can come and beat me over the head with the National Curriculum folders if they so wish, but they can also come and show me how to do it if they don't like the way I do it.

A fourth approach is to *stand back* and then get on with it *if* necessary, with the minimum of fuss. Harriet adopts this approach if a new proposal conflicts with what she thinks is right.

> I wait and see if I have to do it. I've had no problems with the National Curriculum. I have a lot of problems with assessment,

And of course we do it like this.

Figure 7.1: We can quietly go away and put ourselves right

but I don't fight it because I don't think there's any percentage in saying, 'Isn't it dreadful?' You're just losing emotional energy. I say, 'OK, let's make the best of a bad job,' so there's a minimal impact on everybody: children, teachers and the school.

The following interview with Rita illustrates a fifth strategy which is to *be realistic* about what you can do and the rate at which you can do it.

Anne: But changes in the curriculum and things don't bother you?

Rita: No, not really, not really because I think everything has to be implemented at a reasonable pace and you can only go as fast as you can go. So I suppose — I mean, sometimes I get a panic on and think, 'I should be doing this because, you know, it says so here,' but generally speaking, I don't feel that way.

Anne: So you don't feel the pressure that some people say from the government or anything; you just do what you can?

Rita: Yes, I think so. I think so. Yes, I try and do the best that I can and that's all you can say. I think if you're putting in the hours and you're doing your best, then you can't argue with that.

Anne: How long have you been teaching?

Rita: About ten years.

Anne: So you know that it's all right to do that.

Rita: I suppose so. Maybe that's what it is. Yes, probably if you were talking to me about six years ago it would be a different story, but maybe that's it.

And, finally, Katrina feels that it is important to *believe in your actions and keep an open mind*. She went on to explore how this came about for her.

Something I used to find stressful, but I don't any more, which is interesting: it was when I was having to question my own philosophy, the way in which I'm seeing education and thinking about how I should be teaching and the children should be learning. I used to find it extremely stressful if somebody questioned what I was doing or threw it back at me. You know, 'Are you sure about that?' 'Should you be doing that?' I feel much happier living with ambiguity now, and uncertainty, and the fact that I'm never going to get it sussed; that all I can do is try and do the best with what I know and understand now and make sure that I keep up to date with current research and try and keep an open mind. I don't want to get a fixed philosophy, I want to have an open mind and, as I say, I used to find that stressful if it was threatening my whole philosophy. But I don't so much now. Maybe it's because that's become part of my philosophy, living with ambiguity.

A Couple of Reflections

Iona rather wistfully remarked,

> I expect younger people find changes easier because they tend to be more adaptable and they didn't know what it was like before.

She might be reassured that some of the younger members of the profession admire their older colleagues for their tenacity.

> I mean, you think to yourself, 'Why do people keep on doing it?' I mean, there are all sorts of rewards as well, but it is just such a different job from the job ten years ago. I mean, what it must be like for those poor people who started 20-odd years ago — I really don't know how they cope with it.

The other point I want to make before leaving the subject is that, if you like, this whole book could be seen as a recommendation to change! That, I can assure you, is not its prime intention. Certainly it presents possible strategies for you to try but it is entirely up to you whether you take them on board or not. Indeed — as discussed above — if you personally are not convinced by them, you are unlikely to become less stressed by endeavouring to incorporate any of the suggestions into your life and practice.

To summarise, the complexities involved in change should not be underestimated but, with vision, commitment, courage, understanding and time, your efforts may well be rewarded!

Summary

- Making changes can be disruptive and difficult.
- Changes generally involve you taking a risk.
- Effective change requires your commitment to the idea.
- Initially, making a change to one aspect of your performance can affect your performance in others.
- Effective change takes time.
- When you make changes in school others may well be affected and may resist your plans.
- Imposed change can be particularly difficult to accommodate. Its success depends on your attitude to it, your understanding of it, how well it fits in with what you already do and your feelings of control over it.
- The imposition of the National Curriculum was generally well received but created a lot of chaos and required a tremendous dedication and effort on the part of many teachers?
- Change may be facilitated through careful timing; an unhurried, sensitive approach; discussion and consensus as a staff; a detached and realistic attitude; a belief in your actions and an open mind!

Further Reading and References

If you are interested in studying educational change in greater detail you might like to read:

CLAXTON, G. (1989) *Being a Teacher: A Positive Approach to Change and Stress*, London, Cassell.

The texts referred to in this chapter were:

FEIMAN-NEMSER, S. and LODEN, R.E. (1986) 'The cultures of teaching', in WITTROCK, M.C. (ed.) *Handbook of Research on Teaching, 3rd edition*, New York, Macmillan.
GREENO, J.C. (1980) 'Psychology of learning, 1960–1980: One participant's observations', *American Psychologist*, **35**, pp.713–28.
KAMII, C. (1985) *Young Children Reinvent Arithmetic*, New York, Teachers' College Press.

LAAR, B., BLATCHFORD, R., WINKLEY, D., BADMAN, G. and HOWARD, R. (1989) *Effective Teaching*, Oxford, National Primary Centre.

NICHOLLS, A. (1983) *Managing Educational Innovations*, London, Allen and Unwin.

RUDDUCK, J. (1991) *Innovation and Change*, Buckingham, Open University Press.

SHRESHLY, W. and BERND, M. (1992) 'School reform: Real improvement takes time', *Journal of School Leadership*, **3**, pp.320–9.

YAPP, N. (1987) *Bluff Your Way in Teaching*, Horsham, Ravette Books.

SECTION III
Life Beyond Teaching

Quite simply, there is more to life than one's job. The sooner we all appreciate that the sooner we will begin to live more fulfilling lives. This chapter is an attempt to open up some of the possibilities . . .

8 Life Beyond Teaching

Not long ago a member of my family was seriously ill. During that time I found I became very focused and single-minded. Her needs came first and I suppose, purely out of necessity, I paid some attention to my own but nothing else was important. I was what my partner called 'out of it'. Fortunately people were very understanding and no one took offence at my distraction, but what if it had gone on?

When people become totally wrapped up in their job I strongly suspect that they feel and behave much as I did, but until they stand back they may not even be aware of the fact. It's a bit like a see-saw where, at one end, your preoccupation (often your job) totally weighs you down and, at the other end, other aspects of your life barely get a look in.

This chapter is about the quality of life. It is not about 'doing okay': most people are pretty good at that. It is about enhancing your life not only because life is short. Or even that you can prepare for retirement. But more so that you can really experience the satisfaction and richness of being a human being and even — if you like — so that you can become a better teacher as a result! Erich Fromm is once said to have gone so far as to say,

> The aim of life is to live it intensely, to be fully born, to be fully awake.

Rivers and Waterfalls

In some ways you can liken each of us to a river. Most of us, I suspect, are rather like a stream which has got somewhat blocked up with twigs and branches *et cetera*: water can get by but not at full flow. Some people become totally clogged up and in time the resulting dam may well burst, creating all manner of chaos and destruction. Living a more complete and fulfilled life does not, I suggest, imply discarding the twigs and branches but rather letting them move with us as we flow along freely. At the risk of stretching the metaphor, may I further suggest that our river is full of fish and all manner of interesting bits and pieces. The twigs and branches are the inevitable problems which crop up in life and which help us grow. The fish, plants and other paraphernalia are the people, events and experiences which enhance our lives in all manner of fascinating and enjoyable ways.

At one point I was going to discuss how one could release the branches to enable them to flow freely but, in essence, that is what most of the book has been about. Certainly I could talk more about finding time to fit everything into your life; coping with your commitments and responsibilities and so on and so forth. But, instead, I think it is time to introduce a few waterfalls, the aim of which is to stimulate and encourage the flow.

Part of the problem is that when you, I, or anyone else is intensely involved in his/her life, it is very difficult to stand back and take a good look at what is going on and actually see the wood for the trees. Accordingly I have adopted three rather different ways which might prompt you to look at your current state and potential as a more fulfilled human being.

In passing, I should note that, intentionally, I have omitted any reference to personal relationships. There are several reasons for this. One of the most important is that, at times, I feel a real novice in this department: there seems to be so much to learn with each new encounter! Secondly, there are already volumes written on the subject. (Incidentally, for those of you who sometimes feel that members of the opposite sex behave as if they are from another planet, I can recommend Gray (1992) *Men are from Mars, Women are from Venus.*) And then, of course, this book is about you and, in particular, how you can ease the stresses and strains of *your* life without necessarily being dependent on anyone else.

Hemispheres Apart

While it would be inappropriate to provide a full course in anatomy and physiology, a quick sortie into neuropsychology might prove helpful. Basically, everyone has two distinct but, almost without exception, joined halves to their brain: the right and left hemisphere. To a greater or lesser extent — depending on the individual — each half performs various different functions. Which half does what is usually associated with handedness. Thus, for example, right-handed people usually have a 'dominant' left hemisphere and left-handed people have a dominant right. That, in itself, is not particularly important in this discussion; what is important is that the two halves make a whole. This, in effect, means that one of your hemispheres controls most of your language: as a right-hander, when you speak, the likelihood is that your left hemisphere is doing most of the work. Indeed, it is probably true to say of many people that the language (or dominant) side of their brain does considerably more than the other hemisphere. That is not to say that the minor hemisphere is any less able than its dominant partner but, I suspect, for many of us it is considerably underused. When, for example, did you last really use your artistic or musical talents? You might be one of many who laugh and shrug, saying, 'What artistic or musical talents?' Perhaps you are not a budding Leonardo or Ludwig but what's wrong with a good bellow in the bath or on the way to work in the car now and again! Indeed, who is to say that you have no talent?

One common misconception, Betty Edwards (1988) would argue, is that relatively few people can draw. She believes that everyone is artistic but that many do not appreciate the fact because, in all probability, their potential was stifled at an early age. Even I, with only a little encouragement, have learnt to draw a bit and that — I can assure you — is certainly saying something! If you do not believe me, try reading Betty Edwards' book referenced at the end of the chapter.

Teacher–learner, Parent–child

Here I thought we could take time to consider who you are and the numerous roles you play. By this I am not implying that your life is full of pretence! Rather, I am making the point that at school you are generally a teacher but in other places and at other times you might be an aunt or uncle, a gardener, a golfer or what-have-you. Some people will see you as 'their teacher'. Others may perceive you as 'their next-door neighbour', their 'partner', their 'child', and so on. Try making a list of all the roles you play but avoid too much fine detail or the list might be endless. If you find that there is some overlapping between roles, use the more time-consuming aspect for your list or refine your terms. For example, as a parent you may spend a lot of time as a cleaner and therefore you might subdivide being a parent into a cleaning role and a parenting role when you are, for example, nurturing your relationship with your child. Then order the time spent in each role. For example, your original list might read: 'teacher, sailor, novel reader, cook, cleaner, archer'. On re-ordering, it might become: 'teacher, cook, cleaner, novel reader, archer, sailor'. Then ask yourself the following questions:

- Are you happy in each role? If not, can you do something about it? (As discussed previously, cleaners are a surprisingly inexpensive essential for some people, as can be ironers, gardeners etc.)

- How do you feel about the time you devote to each role? As you are a teacher you would expect to spend a lot of your time on the job but does that leave very little time for anything else? You may also find that commitments at home — such as being a parent or carer — take up considerable time. Perhaps, as a single parent, that may be the way it has to be, but there may be ways to combine or adjust roles. You could, for example, try teaming up with someone in a similar position and pursue your hobby together or separately, depending on whether you can take the children along or whether one of you has to babysit while the other goes out and about.

- Would you like other things on the list? By way of suggestion, do you fancy becoming a singer, a hang-glider or ballroom dancer? What is seriously stopping your giving it a go!

- Some of your roles involve other players: have you considered taking another part now and again? As a teacher you are surrounded by learners. I expect you find that you too learn but how often are you in the more formal role of learner? How often do you experience the thrill of learning new and exciting things at the hands of a challenging and exciting teacher?

- As a parent, how often, if ever, do you take the role of child and let someone care for and nurture you? You might not want to, of course, or you might not know how to go about organizing it. Perhaps, in part, this is because you are thinking too narrowly. You may well imagine that you do not know anyone who could take on that role but — as will be discussed more fully in the next section — there are professionals, such as aromatherapists, reflexologists, beauticians, who can fulfil this nurturing role surprisingly effectively.

- You might also like to prefix each role with an adjective. Try to do so spontaneously and observe your reactions in the process. Such an exercise may well result in two people interpreting similar lists entirely differently: one might consider herself to be a useful helper and general team member while the other might feel that she is a skivvy and a frustrated leader. Obviously I cannot predict your reactions but are you happy with them? If not, it may be relatively easy to do something about your roles, your attitudes towards them, or both. As has been so often suggested in this book, perhaps you could talk to someone — either a friend or a professional — about it. Or take a course in assertiveness training to increase your self-esteem, enable you to take a more pro-active role in life and explore Eleanor Roosevelt's view that, 'No one can make you feel inferior without your consent'.

- Finally, at the beginning of this section I said that I was not implying that your life was full of pretence but was I wrong in my assumption? If it is and — assuming you are doing nothing illegal or harmful — you are happy with it, then I guess that is fine. Suffice to say that I have discovered I save a lot of energy by being as honest as I can be without causing offence. It may sometimes require some diplomacy and nerve but it seems to conserve limited resources and minimize future complications: for, as Sir Walter Scott said, 'Oh what a tangled web we weave when first we practice to deceive!'

Body, Mind and Soul

'Body, mind and soul' is a relatively common expression but how often do we really examine it? I am not suggesting that we become metaphysical here: if you wish to pursue that line of thinking I can refer you to my brother who, as a philosopher, is happy to explore such issues! Rather, I think, we sometimes need to consider whether we really cherish and attend to each of these aspects of our being.

To stay alive we need to take a certain amount of care of our bodies. We all know that we should not smoke or drink too heavily, or abuse our bodies by lack of exercise or sleep, or eat fattening foods and so on and so forth. The problem often is that it is usually people who do all the right things who make these statements; rarely do they appreciate how hard it is to 'mend the error of our ways' even if we profess that it is the right thing to do.

I am not qualified to talk about addiction but there are some addresses and references at the end of the chapter which might prove helpful. I can, however, speak from observation and personal experience on the problems of taking adequate exercise. Having been fairly energetic in my youth, I found that by my late thirties I was taking next to no exercise. I knew all the propaganda about exercise making you healthier, more efficient and generally more alive and on top of things but I never seemed to have the energy to do something about it. I am not saying that I have entirely won the battle but there have certainly been some effective inducements to get me started, namely:

- a bike ride to the pub 20 minutes away;
- an attractive swimming pool where one can go with friends;
- regular Tai Chi classes which have been paid for in advance!
- (to my surprise) a game of rounders with my colleagues;
- sunny weather;
- large expanses of Norfolk coastline;
- a garden where the weeds flourish but which does not scream for attention and seems to thrive on the efforts of an unskilled labourer.

All of these activities I enjoy and that, I think, is crucial. What is the point of sweating away at something you loathe when, in the same time and with considerably less mental effort, you could be doing something you enjoy? There are all manner of ways in which one can take exercise. Alix Kirsta (1986), for example, divides the possibilities into six broad categories: aerobic dance, aerobic exercise (this includes running, swimming, cycling and fast walking), calisthenics, yoga, weight machines and martial arts. One thing to watch is that you don't overdo it! Donald Norfolk explains the need to,

> Pace yourself. Take a break before you tire. Many people who have adopted aerobic exercise programmes have been disappointed to find that instead of feeling fresher after their strenuous work-outs they seem more exhausted than ever before. The reason is that they are often pushing themselves *too* hard . . . What's the point of wasting energy getting fit, if you never arrive at the point when you actually *feel* fit? (1985, pp.116–17)

Apart from the sheer enjoyment of exercise, the good news is that there comes a time when you actually want to do it!

There are numerous books available on nutrition, diet, food allergies etc., etc. The papers are also full of what we should and shouldn't eat and drink: one minute we are told that we shouldn't touch a drop of alcohol and the next we are being encouraged to drink red wine because it helps prevent heart disease. That being said, I suspect most people reading this will know which foods are said to be good for you and which are not. We are, however, human. If you thoroughly enjoy eating healthy food all the time, then lucky you! If, however, you hanker after a bag of chips or a packet of sweets from time to time, is that so terrible? If that is *all* you hanker after then you may indeed have a problem but I would have thought that the pleasure gained from the occasional cake or two far outweighs the more negative aspects of the misdemeanour. The secret seems to be moderation and balance while keeping a relaxed — but not comatose — eye on your weight and any adverse reactions. (By these I mean allergies or other inconvenient problems such as the 'high' and subsequent 'slump' which chocolate often induces.)

So much for basic body maintenance: this chapter is about enhancing the quality of your life, not just keeping things ticking over. For most of you it is almost certainly time that you gave your body a treat! Some treats are usually easily arranged, such as — if it appeals — a long hot bath rather than the typical quick dip with the statutory wash behind the ears. In this category also comes the gentle massaging of your face, particularly round the eyes and temple area. More organization might be required for a session of aromatherapy or reflexology. Both can be wonderfully relaxing and beneficial but only — in the case of the latter — if you have no aversion to someone touching your feet! Deep relaxation or the Alexander Technique are other treats which might appeal. For further information on these and other strategies I suggest you read *The HEA Guide to Complementary Medicines and Therapies* (see end of chapter).

As already alluded to above, our minds and bodies are in very close interaction. Indeed, I remember being startled when a general practitioner once told me that he thought about 70 per cent of the complaints he saw were, in some way, related to his patients' state of mind. He was in no way implying that most of his patients were psychiatric cases but simply making the point that stress frequently induces health problems and vice versa.

Most of this book has been about our minds and the state they are in so I will not dwell on them too long here. But take a moment to pause and consider whether you attend to your mind in a way that enhances the quality of your life. Do you, for example, ever find yourself intellectually challenged or really excited by a new concept or idea? Does anything totally absorb your mind in such a way that — not only are your cares and worries temporarily forgotten — you thoroughly enjoy the mental exercise and get a real buzz out of the experience? Many people find this with games such as chess or bridge. Others enjoy attending lectures, battling with crosswords or reading a riveting novel or biography. Evening classes can prove to be another source of stimulating and satisfying mental exercise. One of the great things about my recently discovered Tai Chi class mentioned earlier is that it provides mental and physical exercise without my blowing a gasket or waking up as stiff as a board the next day.

Such suggestions may seem horrifying — or even insulting — after you have spent a very challenging day at school. This is certainly not the intention and I am not proposing that you plough your way through *War and Peace* in a week. (Incidentally, I found it a surprisingly satisfying read but, I can assure you, it is not something I would want to tackle when I only had a spare five or ten minutes here or there.) What I am suggesting is that your mind — like your body — might appreciate some more recreational exercise now and again and would almost certainly work better as a result.

And now on to the third part of the triad: your soul. Here the controversy could really start for I am well aware that some people do not believe in the entity many call a 'soul'. The term 'spirit', I gather, is more acceptable but, rather than be side-tracked by these particular words, let me try to capture the sense using other terms such as your very essence or your vital being. I find it hard, in fact, to put something so essential and fundamental into words. It is something, I suspect, that most of us often neglect and yet it is at the very heart of the human experience. T.S. Eliot posed the question, 'Where is the life we have lost in living?' and it is this, I think, that each and every one of us should endeavour to answer for ourselves.

It is about appreciation: appreciating aspects of life which, in our haste, we rarely, if ever, notice. It could be something we might call commonplace until we take the time to look at it, such as a spider's web on a winter's day. Or it could be something rather more dramatic such as the crashing of the waves during a storm. Kirsta puts it rather differently, saying that it is,

> . . . important to learn how to waste time creatively . . . Giving yourself a break to laze, day-dream, or play, calms your body and mind, recharges your energy, and inspires optimism, contentment, and humour. (1986, p.76)

Basically it is about nurturing your inner self by taking time — it may only be a matter of seconds — to enjoy art, music, a glorious day, being alive. Some use meditation, others religion, others a quiet time to stop and reflect on the beauty around them. You may use all three, you may have your own approach, or you may have little time and patience with what might be perceived as a self-indulgent, esoteric concept. That is your right and, in my view, your loss. Take five minutes looking at the stars and perhaps you will see what I mean.

Postscript

In some ways *Teaching Under Pressure* was not an easy book to write because I was trying to cater for so many different people with a range of experiences and expertise. In other ways it was easy thanks to the generosity and honesty of those many teachers, headteachers and deputies who gave of their thoughts, advice and that precious commodity, time.

There is no doubt about it: at its best teaching is a challenging and extremely rewarding profession. There is little to beat the tremendous satisfaction of seeing a child's face light up when, at last, they understand. There is, however, more to life than teaching and we, as teachers, must remember that. And, on that note, let me leave you with some advice from Yvonne Gold and Robert Roth:

> Life is not always fair or pleasant; roll with the bad and rejoice with the good. (1993, p.196)

And from Anne Dickson:

> When making a list of things to do, add at least one pleasurable activity for yourself so that the importance of taking care of yourself doesn't entirely escape your notice. (1994, April 22)

Further Reading and References

Three entirely different books all of which explore, in effect, life beyond teaching are:

CARNEGIE, D. (1990) *How to Stop Worrying and Start Living*, London, Cedar.
(This book was originally published in 1953 but is fresh, full of examples and written in an easy Americanized style.)

FROMM, E. (1978) *To Have or To Be?*, London, Abacus.
(This is a very interesting and thought-provoking book but it is not what I would describe as light reading.)

ROWE, D. (1991) *Wanting Everything: The Art of Happiness*, London, Harper Collins.
(Dorothy Rowe is a psychologist who has published widely. The authoress, Fay Weldon, would like to see this particular book 'on every bookshelf in the country'.)

Should you wish to explore various therapies you might find the following a useful starting point:

HEALTH EDUCATION AUTHORITY (1994) *The HEA Guide to Complementary Medicines and Therapies*, London, Health Education Authority.

If you feel you need help with an addiction I suggest:

SWEET, C. (1994) *Off the Hook: How to Enjoy Living an Addiction-free Life*, London, Piatkus Books.

The following books were referred to in the text:

DICKSON, A. (1994) *A Book of Your Own*, London, Quartet Books.
EDWARDS, B. (1986) *Drawing on the Artist Within*, London, Fontana.
GRAY, J. (1992) *Men are from Mars, Women are from Venus*, London, Thorsons.
GOLD, Y. and ROTH, R.A. (1993) *Teachers Managing Stress and Preventing Burnout: The Professional Health Solution*, London, Falmer Press.
KIRSTA, A. (1986) *The Book of Stress Survival*, London, Unwin Paperbacks.
NORFOLK, D. (1985) *Farewell to Fatigue*, London, Pan Books.

Useful Addresses

Action on Smoking and Health (ASH)
109 Gloucester Place
London W1H 3PH
0171–935 3519

Alcoholics Anonymous (AA) — General information
PO Box 1, Stonebow House
Stonebow
York Y01 2NJ
01904 – 644026

British Association for Psychotherapists
37 Mapesbury Road
London NW2 4HJ
0181– 452 9823

Eating Disorders Association
Sackville Place
44 Magdalen Street
Norwich NR3 1JE
01603 – 621414

Gamblers Anonymous
PO Box 88
London SW10 0ED

Narcotics Anonymous
UK Service Office
PO Box 1980
London N19 3LS
0171–272 9040

Relate
Herbert Gray College
Little Church Street
Rugby CV21 3AP
01788–573241

Samaritans (Central Office)
46 Marshall Street
London W1V 1LR
0171–734 2800

Index

R